George's Generations:
Through The Magic Doors

By

Gavin Hodgson

George's Generations

First Edition. March 2019
ISBN: 978-1-9160808-5-0

Edited by Coleman Editing
www.colemanediting.co.uk

Cover design and interior by Ebook Launch
www.ebooklaunch.com

Published by Gavin Hodgson

gavinhodgson.co.uk

Dedicated to my late Grandma Iris,
Grandad Thomas, Aunt Alice,
Aunt Emma, Aunt Lorraine and
Aunt Pamela

CONTENTS

Prologue

It was July 26th, 1986, the start of the school summer holidays, and in the small village of Meadow View in the North of England, there lived a boy named George Rainbow.

Meadow View was situated deep in the countryside, surrounded by moorland, rolling fields, hills, and a quarry located on the other side of a large forest. It was a small, relatively quiet place where everybody knew everybody else.

A typical 10-year-old boy, George lived in a small three-bedroom house with his two brothers - Sean, who was 12, and David, who was 14 - and his parents, Cherry and

John, with most of his extended family living in the same village.

Just down the road lived his grandma and grandad, and across from them his great aunt Alice. On the outskirts of the village lived his great aunt Emma, and at the top of the village lived George's dad's two older sisters. As neither of them had ever married, they lived in the same house together. His dad said they were 'thick as thieves' together.

George's grandma, grandad, Auntie Alice and Auntie Emma all favoured George; whenever he would go around to Grandma and Grandad's house they would always fuss over him, asking him how he and his friends were doing and telling him to look after himself. He would always get a big hug and a kiss from his grandma, while his grandad would hug him before shaking his hand and calling him his 'mate'.

He was an adventurous and daring soul, who always loved playing outdoors and doing all the things that 10-year-old boys normally enjoy doing: climbing trees, making hideouts, playing with his friends and just enjoying being free from school throughout the holidays. As soon as he was up in the morning he was out into the big, wide world - and he wouldn't come back until it was time to be fed or go to bed.

Like most young boys he'd much rather play with his friends than his brothers, particularly as they were older and always picking on him. They often got him into trouble, persuading him to do them favours and lie for them to his parents.

Chapter One

The School Summer Holidays

It was a bright, sunny Saturday morning and my first day of the school summer holidays - my favourite time of year! This particular morning was the beginning of another red-hot summer's day, and the sun woke me up, shining through a crack in my bedroom curtains.

I was tired for a second or two, my brain still foggy with sleep, but after a quick stretch I jumped up out of bed and quickly pulled the curtains open, revealing a clear blue sky above the rooftops of the village.

What a great day to play out, I thought.

Eager to get outside and on with the day, as quickly as I could I got dressed and went downstairs, where my mum was already up and making herself a cup of tea.

She was always the first up in the morning, opening the curtains and windows and getting the house ready for a new day.

"Good morning, Mum!" I said.

"Morning, George," she replied. "Do you want your breakfast?"

"Yes, please," I responded, so she made me jam on toast with just the right amount of butter underneath - my favourite.

As I sat there munching on my toast and gazing out of the window, wondering what I and my friends would get up to that day, Mum was pottering around the kitchen, listening to the TV that was on in the next room. I began to listen to the news reporter as my mind began to wander. She was speaking with a very excited astronomer from an observatory halfway across the world, in Australia.

They were discussing a large increase in solar flare activity that had erupted on the surface of the sun the day before, and what impact these would have on the planets night sky. The astronomer explained that they were expecting to see the Southern Lights across their night skies, which wasn't that unusual, given that it was winter in the Southern hemisphere. However, the increase in activity would also prompt the Northern Lights to make an appearance, which was an unusual event for the summer months. The reporter said that people in Britain might be able to see them in the next few nights as far south as the Midlands.

I turned and looked at the TV, interested. "Mum, what are the Northern Lights?" I asked.

"The Aurora Borealis," she replied and went on, when it was clear that I didn't understand, "it's a phenomenon also known as the Northern Lights, where great ribbons of green and blue charged particles flow through the upper atmosphere, turning the sky green. It's caused when huge radioactive explosions take place on the surface of the sun, causing solar flares."

"Wow," I said.

"The flares travel through space and hit the Earth's atmosphere, causing a reaction that triggers the Northern Lights. Apparently it's the most beautiful natural phenomena you will ever see, but I very much doubt it'll come this far down."

"You never know Mum, it might," I said excitedly, hoping that it would.

I took the last few bites of my breakfast and brushed the toast crumbs off my hands. "I'm off out now," I told my mum.

"Okay," she said. "Play carefully and remember, you must come in when you hear me shouting."

"Okay. Bye then, Mum!" I shouted as I left the house.

I went around to call on my friends Thomas and Paul, who lived a few doors away from each other, just down the road from me.

Our parents always told us that we must remain in earshot and not to travel too far away from home, so they could find us if they needed to, and that we must always stick together.

The first instruction we found difficult to stick to, but we never had a problem sticking together as we were best friends. Thomas, Paul and I went everywhere and did everything as a group and on this morning we decided to go to the quarry on the far side of the woods.

The quarry was a huge expanse of water that had been there for over 60 years, It was about the size of two football fields or more, with a steep drop into the water of about six foot on one side, but shallower on the other. About halfway around, where the drop to the water was shallower, there were trees, bushes and open areas with long grass that flowed majestically to and fro in the wind. In good weather the sun would shine on it all day long. It was paradise. A lovely, peaceful place to be, with only the wind blowing through the trees and grasses, the birds singing, and no sound of the hustle or bustle from the village.

But, of course, this was a place we were not allowed to play! Our parents always told us of the dangers of the quarry - the long drops and the water - and reminded us that over the long history of the place three boys had drowned in the quarry. Their bodies had never been found, which made them a favourite subject among the older boys when they told ghost stories to scare little brothers.

10-year-old me didn't understand why they worried though. I was, I thought, far too clever to fall in and drown. We were always careful when we played around the edge, but still our parents fretted and scolded and we weren't allowed to go there. So, of course, we snuck down there without them finding out instead.

When we got to the water's edge we would throw stones into the deep quarry pool, and whoever could throw their stone the furthest was the winner for that day.

Occasionally we threw a plastic bottle in there and would try to hit it with our stones. It was such a simple game, yet we could happily spend hours on it. It was such fun! Occasionally, we would bring our slingshots, for greater distance and accuracy.

Every now and then we would go up to the old disused railway line above the quarry, where we would collect lumps of iron ore. These were small, heavy, misshapen ball bearings that worked really well as ammunition for our slingshots. This was much more fun, and we could get them so much further across the water than the stones.

That day we played for hours, just laughing and having fun, but because we knew we weren't supposed to be there, every now and then we would stop and listen carefully for our parents shouting for us to come in as we were supposed to remain in earshot and down at the quarry we were a little bit too far away.

Eventually, we gave up. The sun was high in the sky now, so we knew hours must have had passed, and we had heard nothing from our parents.

"I have to go in now," Paul said. "We're going to see my grandma in hospital, but I'll be out again tomorrow."

"Okay then, let's walk up," I said as we threw the last of the stones into the quarry.

On our way home I spotted my brothers walking towards us across the old football field. I guessed they were looking for me.

"Where have you been?" Sean asked.

"Nowhere!" I told him, as we met in the middle. "We've just been playing in the woods on the rope swing."

"What rope swing?" he asked suspiciously. He looked from one to the other of us, but none of us betrayed a thing.

"There is no rope swing down there. Mum's been shouting for you for the last 20 minutes."

"We must've been playing too loud, I guess," I said.

"You better not have been down the quarry," he told me. "I'll tell Dad if you have."

"There's no need to tell Dad anything."

I waved goodbye to Thomas and Paul and said, "I better go in before I get into trouble."

When I walked through the door, straightaway my dad asked me where I'd been.

"Your mum has been shouting for you for the last 20 minutes," he said, cross. "She was worried."

"We've just been playing over the field, by the trees, on the rope swing. I couldn't hear her," I lied.

"You better not let me find out you've been playing down the quarry, or you'll be grounded for the whole summer holidays," Dad threatened.

"I wasn't," I said.

"Well, I'm just saying you better not!"

Deep down I think he knew I was down there; he just couldn't prove it. I got away with it that time.

"Get washed up for dinner, then come back down," he said.

When I sat at the table Sean and David looked over and said, "We know you were down the quarry."

I stared at them. How could they have known? "Don't tell Dad," I pleaded.

"Okay, but you owe us," they replied, looking pleased with themselves.

That was usually a bad thing in my experience, but it was still better than getting into trouble with my dad.

Just then Mum brought our dinners in from the kitchen and placed them down on the table. She ruffled my hair as she passed my chair and went to get another couple of plates.

"Chicken dinner - my favourite! Thanks Mum," I said - and meant it. I had worked up quite an appetite.

Dad, who had come in behind her with the cutlery and salt and pepper narrowed his eyes at Sean. "What did you just say to George?"

"Nothing," he replied.

"It's important you don't go down the quarry, boys," he said again. "It's far too dangerous!"

"Why, Dad?" I asked, wanting to hear a ghost story about a drowned boy, like the ones Sean and David would tell me, trying to frighten me.

Dad sat down, a frown on his face. "When I was about your age, I met some boys down the quarry," he said. "One of them was called George, like you," he nodded in my direction. "And the other one…" He tutted at himself. "I can't for the life of me think of his name. Anyway, it was just before our school summer holidays when I first met George, the day after your Aunt Pamela's birthday, and when we met, we became good friends straight away."

Mum came in with her own plate and a jug of water and motioned for us all to start eating while Dad told us his story.

"We were always challenging each other to do silly things - you know, who could climb the highest, or run the farthest, whatever. The way you boys all do with your friends." He looked at the three of us and sighed. "One day when we were out playing by the water I came up with this ridiculous, pointless, and highly dangerous challenge. I wish

I'd never thought of it. "I tied a tight rope across the quarry wall and challenged the others and myself to walk as close to the water as we could without getting our feet wet.

"As dangerous and stupid as it was, we did it anyway and things very quickly went horribly wrong. I nearly fell in and he pulled me back. He saved my life that day - and not just the once, either. He was always pulling me out of trouble - but that day was the worst. And it was my idea, so it was my fault."

He rubbed a hand over his face.

"George was a good friend to me, and that's who we named you after," he told me, much to my surprise.

"I didn't know one of the drowned boys was your friend... and I never knew I was named after him," I gasped.

Dad nodded. "Anyway, like I'm telling you - the same as my dad told me - you shouldn't play down there. Because this wasn't the first time something bad happened. Two boys also drowned there 30 years before George did."

Mum took his hand for a moment and he gave her a sad smile.

"But we didn't listen," Dad continued. "When me and my friends played together we thought we were big and clever, like all kids do. We thought we could never get hurt, that we were invincible. But we weren't."

"What happened then?" David asked.

"Like I said, one day I decided to tie the long rope we had found from one side of the wall to the other, just above the water," Dad continued. "As far as we knew it had never been done before, so it seemed like an excellent challenge."

"Is that how you got the scar on your head?" Sean interrupted.

"No," he said, touching it lightly with his fingers. "But I did get it down the quarry a few days earlier."

"How?" I asked, peering at the faded scar on the side of his head. I'd seen it so many times before, but I'd never thought where it might have come from. Neither, from the sounds of it, had my brothers.

An odd look came over Dad's face. "Well, it was the strangest thing," he told us slowly. "I was playing on the bankside when a rock came out of nowhere and hit me on the head. Split the skin open - that's how I got the scar."

"Who threw it?" Mum asked, interested.

"I don't know, but I threw it back hoping to hit whoever it was."

We all laughed.

"Anyway," he went on, with a mixture of excitement about being able to share these tales of his youth, but also sadness at losing a friend. "Halfway across the wall I slipped and started sliding down towards the water. I panicked and shouted for George to help. Just then, he grabbed me by the arm and stopped me from falling in - but we both struggled as he tried to pull me up. We were both panicking and scared.

"I really thought I was going to fall in!" Dad's voice quavered, which was unsettling. I had never seen him afraid before. "Just as I managed to get my footing, George lost his and slid past me, banging his head on the wall and falling into the water head first."

All four of us had stopped eating now - myself, my brothers and my mum - all of us enthralled by the story, and by the fact that it had happened to Dad (though it was possible Mum had heard the story before). I hadn't even really imagined him as a child before, but here he was, reliving the worst moment of his life.

"I turned to try and catch him, but it was too late," he said, tears welling up in his eyes as he spoke. "George quickly slipped under the surface and there was nothing I could do to save him.

"I jumped in and swam around the area where he fell, but there was nothing. The water is so deep there, I couldn't see him - I couldn't find him anywhere," Dad said, and I could tell he was still angry and upset about the events of that day, even though they had happened so long ago. "I swam to the edge and climbed out, and ran around the whole quarry looking for him. I kept shouting his name, but he was nowhere to be found. He'd gone - he'd drowned."

I swallowed, truly understanding for the first time in my life why he and Mum were always so strict about us not going near the water. But his story wasn't over yet.

"I ran home as fast as I could and told my parents what had happened," he went on. "They were worried that the same thing could have happened to me and angry that I'd been playing near the quarry, but they quickly called for the police and a huge search party - including police divers and everyone from the village - went over to the quarry and started looking for him.

"Divers went under the water with lights, but the water was too murky and deep and they couldn't find him," Dad told us. "They brought out police dogs and handlers - which were still pretty new then - and they sniffed around the bankside in case he'd climbed out and was lying injured in the long grass, or something."

Dad paused and took a long drink of the water Mum had poured out for him. "It was so sad and tragic," he recalled. "And eventually the police reluctantly concluded that he had most likely drowned. They spent the next three or four days searching for his body, but were unable to find it anywhere. They had experts come out and assess the quarry, but they said he had probably sunk into the soft mud beneath the water and it would be too dangerous for anyone to try and recover his body." His frown deepened a touch. "He's probably still down there, somewhere."

He rubbed tears away from his eyes and I exchanged worried glances with my brothers. We had never seen him cry before. He must have been really close to one of the dead boys - and we had never known, in all the years we had told and retold the ghost stories.

"Who were his parents, what did they say?" David asked. "I bet they were devastated!"

"That's one of the sad things," Dad told him. "We never did find his parents and no boy was ever reported missing. The police thought he might be a runaway. Maybe he fell out with his parents and just ran away. Such a sad end to a short and probably quite sad life." He sighed heavily and looked up at us again. "And this is why I don't want you playing down the quarry."

He quickly rubbed his eyes, sniffed, and sat up straight in his chair. "Right, no more talk of the past tonight."

"But what about the other boys?" I asked, interested.

"Yeah," said Sean, "the ones who drowned there 30 years before-" He paused, catching Mum's expression. "Er... before the story you just told."

"One of them was a friend of your grandma and Aunt Alice's, so you can ask them when you go around to help your grandma weed the garden, like you promised," said Mum. "Now eat up, or it will be stone cold."

Like the boys in the quarry, I thought, but didn't say aloud.

By the time dinner had finished and as the evening drew in, my dad said, "It's time to go to bed. It's getting late."

"What about the Northern Lights?" I asked.

"The Northern Lights?" he echoed, puzzled.

"Yes!" I told him, trying to remember what the astronomer had said. "Mum and I heard it on the news this morning. They said we should see the Northern Lights due to some high solar activity on the sun."

"You will do absolutely anything to avoid going to bed," Dad said, but then he laughed. "Alright, if you want to see the Lights then sit there nice and quiet while I watch the telly, and you can stay up and we can all look for them together."

About an hour and a half later it started to become dark. Soon it was pitch black outside, and a clear night, so all five of us went out into the garden and sat down on a picnic blanket, gazing up into the night sky. Fortunately, it was lovely and warm for that time of night - given the heat of the day - and we rather enjoyed sitting quietly in the garden, staring up at the starry sky, waiting for something to begin.

Just as we were about to give up, I saw a flash of fleeting white-green meander across the sky like a ghost. It was there one moment and gone the next. "Is that it?" I gasped. "I thought I saw something green in the sky."

"No," Mum said - she hadn't seen it. "I thı.. might have imagined it just because you want to see ıt much. Oh..."

But as she was speaking, a big slow-moving flash of green and purple light moved across the sky in a wave, and all five of us gasped.

No one spoke. We simply looked up, following the eerie, beautiful light pass like a slow-moving river across the entire sky. There were other colours mixed in with the green: whites, blues, purples. Mum told us that in other cultures, people used to believe that these were their ancestors, watching over the Earth. I could readily believe it. It was the most amazing thing I'd ever seen, or would ever see again.

Unbeknown to any of us, the water of the quarry lit up, reflecting the emerald shades of the sky above it.

As the waves of colour in the sky grew in intensity, the quarry pool glowed brighter and brighter, the silhouette of the trees alongside becoming darker and darker against it. All of a sudden, arcs of electricity began to jump and dance above the glassy, still surface, travelling rapidly from one bank to another, all around the artificial lake.

These arcs seemed to join together to form one, great spark of blue-green and purple energy, which travelled majestically across the surface of the water, making small electrical cracking sounds as tiny sparks flew off it, hovering above the water for a few seconds before fading.

The great spark of electrical energy reached the centre of the quarry pool, where it drifted closer until the tip of it touched the water. Then, BANG! The spark died with an explosion of air that spread out in all directions from the centre of the pool, blowing harshly through the branches of the trees and grass for a moment, then all was still once more.

As quickly as the Northern Lights came, they went; the green lights faded and the sky became dark once again.

"Well, that was worth a look outside, wasn't it?" Mum said.

Sean and David just shrugged their shoulders, being there age - though they had obviously been just as enthralled as the rest of us.

"It was okay, I suppose," Sean allowed.

Mum replied, "It was fantastic! What about you George? What did you think?"

"I thought it was the most amazing thing I've ever seen," I replied, with complete honestly.

"Good, then we won't have any trouble getting you up to bed now!" She smiled. "Go and brush your teeth and I'll be up in a minute!"

"Night-night," I said to my dad as I went off to bed, visions of a green sky in my head and the story of a drowning boy quite forgotten.

Chapter Two

The Mystery Begins

I woke up early again the next morning, even earlier than the day before, despite how late I'd been allowed to stay up. I turned my head to see the sun shining through the curtains.

What another beautiful day! I thought to myself as I jumped out of bed and pulled the curtains open.

I was still excited and full of energy from seeing the Northern Lights the night before, and I couldn't wait to go and see Paul and Thomas to ask if they had seen the Lights too.

I went downstairs and, as usual, Mum was in the kitchen making a cup of tea.

"Morning," she said, surprised. "You're up earlier than normal. What's the occasion?"

"No occasion," I replied. "I just felt like getting up, that's all."

"What are you up to today?" she asked.

"Me, Thomas and Paul are off down the woods to make a rope swing - I mean, to fix the one we were playing on yesterday. It broke," I added, belatedly recalling the lie I had told about our whereabouts the day before.

"Well, you be careful," she instructed. "We don't want you breaking your arm before you go back to school."

"I'll be fine, Mum," I assured her, "you worry too much."

"That's my job as a mum, to worry," she said. She told me to remember to listen out for her calling me in, and not to be gone too long. "I don't want to have to send Sean and David out looking for you again."

"I know," I mumbled back. I didn't want them to come looking for me either.

With my breakfast in hand, I left the house before my dad or my brothers were up and out of bed. I went to call on my friends but it was still early, and I wasn't sure if they'd be up. When I got to Thomas's house, his curtains were closed. I knew he had a dog called Patch and if I knocked on the door the dog would bark, and I would get them both into trouble, so I just walked on by.

I went to Paul's house, but he didn't have a dog, so despite his curtains also being closed I knocked on the door quite hard. He popped his head out the bedroom window and raised his eyebrows.

"What are you doing out this time of the morning?" he called down to me.

"I just wanted to know if you wanted to go to the quarry," I told him.

"No," he said. "It's too early - and be quiet about the quarry, or my dad will hear you! Come back in an hour."

None of our dads would let any of us play at the quarry, but now I knew why. In a way it made me feel a little guilty about going down there to play - and lying to him, knowing what happened to his friend. But nonetheless, I felt that something was driving me there.

I don't know what it was, it just pulled at me like an invisible magnetic force. Perhaps it was curiosity, or fate, if you like. There was certainly something thrilling about going somewhere forbidden and dangerous - particularly before I knew exactly why it was so risky.

Apart from that, there just was so much to do around there - so much fun to be had. It seemed such a shame to waste it. I just had to make sure none of the adults ever found out what we were up to, and make sure we didn't go the same way as Dad's friend.

So, with a spare hour on my hands before Thomas and Paul would be out of bed and ready for adventure, I decided to have a walk there by myself.

For all my excuses to visit, all the same I knew that I shouldn't go close to the water's edge this morning because I didn't have my friends with me, particularly bearing in mind what my dad had said the night before.

As I got nearer to the quarry pool - not too close, I kept telling myself - I saw a strange haze spread across the water. It was almost like the heat haze you might see on the surface of a road when it's really hot, but I'd never seen a haze like this at the quarry. There was something about it that struck me as odd, too; I couldn't quite put my finger on it.

Beyond the haze, the far side of the quarry looked different. The trees didn't look quite right.

As quickly as it came, the haze faded again and everything looked normal.

I didn't give it much more thought. I was tired after having stayed up late and then woken up earlier than normal, the kind of tiredness that I could have ignored while I was doing something, but as I was at a loose end it came upon me quite suddenly.

I lay down on the bankside and looked up into a sky that had been a beautiful green just the night before, but which today was a deep blue with a few white and fluffy clouds, strewn across it like balls of cotton wool. With the birds singing and the wind blowing through the trees, I laid back and shut my eyes.

As soon as I shut my eyes the whole area went quiet. Through my eyelids, the quality of light around me changed, as if the sun had gone behind a vast cloud. From the direction of the water came a series of odd little cracks, like electricity sparking. I got the weirdest feeling that something odd was happening nearby, but I was in that strange state between waking and sleeping, so I simply assumed it was something to do with whatever dream I was about to fall into.

As if from nowhere, a shockwave like a blast of hot air and static passed through my body. I shot upright in surprise, just in time to see the water of the quarry pool rippling outwards from the centre, as if an enormous stone had been dropped into it. Similarly, the trees and the long grasses billowed, caught in the unnatural breeze.

It stopped abruptly, as if nothing had happened at all, and as soon as it did the birds started singing and the wind rippled gently through the grass.

I felt like I had fallen in a dream and jerked awake, the way that we all do sometimes - except I knew that what I'd seen on waking had been real.

What was that? I thought to myself, heart pounding. I stared around, wondering if I'd dreamed it.

Deciding that I must have done, I laid back down on the bank, enjoying the morning sun and shutting my eyes again. It was very pleasant to be out of doors with nothing in particular to do, listening to the wind blowing through the trees and the birds singing.

These were two of my favourite sounds in the whole world.

Just then, when I was settling back into a doze, all the sounds stopped and for a moment the world went deathly quiet. Then, seconds later I heard girls singing in the distance: "Ring a ring o' roses, a pocketful of posies, a-tishoo, a-tishoo, we all fall down."

Quickly, I sat up and looked around. I couldn't see anything but that mysterious heat haze travelling around the surface of the water. I could clearly hear the girls, though. Their singing was as clear as day. It was almost like they were on the other side of the quarry - but there was no one there.

Were they ghosts? They didn't sound as scary as the ones I'd imagined when my older brothers were trying to frighten me.

As my heart rate increased with excitement and curiosity the birds started singing again and the breeze reclaimed the trees. It was very strange. For those few seconds I didn't feel frightened or anxious - in fact, quite the opposite. I felt somehow very comfortable and warm inside, as if all was right with the world.

As I watched, I was astonished to see the heat haze that had been once again shimmering on the surface of the water slowly disappear.

That was the first time I had ever seen or heard anything like that down at the quarry.

I wonder what it could have been? I thought.

I didn't have a watch to tell the time, but I thought I'd been there long enough now that Paul and Thomas might be up and willing to help me investigate.

I called on Paul first and then we both called on Thomas.

We knocked on his door and his mum answered. "He's still in his pyjamas. He's only just woken up and I'm not surprised, it's only 8 o'clock in the morning!"

Just then, Thomas shouted through, "Come in and I'll get dressed!"

"Come in then, boys," his mum said. "But take off your shoes. I don't want you walking dirt through the house," she warned us.

We went in and up to his bedroom, where I told them both, "While I was waiting for you to get your lazy bums out of bed, I went down to the quarry and when I was there I heard some girls' voices."

"Whose voices were they?" Paul asked.

Generally the girls in our area didn't go up to the quarry.

"I don't know. Just girls, singing some old-fashioned nursery rhyme."

"How old were they?" Thomas asked.

"I don't know," I said, thinking about it. "Maybe our age, or maybe more. I only heard their voices."

Thomas grinned. "We can go down there later and have another look. I don't mind if I get a girlfriend."

"What makes you think one of them would want to go out with you?" Paul asked, and we all laughed.

Paul suggested we go straight down and have a look. Just then, we heard Thomas's mum come up the stairs. She must have heard us because she said, "You're not going down the quarry! You know how your mums and dads feel about this."

"No, Mum," Thomas lied. "We're going down to the woods by the quarry, to make a rope swing!"

"Okay," she said, frowning at us. "But just remember, no playing around the water, please."

"I wonder what happened down there?" he wondered, when she'd gone back downstairs with the laundry.

"I know," I said. "My dad told me the full story last night. I'll tell you on the way."

"I've told my dad that we're going down the woods to make a rope swing, too," Paul said.

Thomas suggested we get a rope out of his dad's shed, then we could actually make a swing.

"That's good," I said. "That way, if David or Sean go down to the woods they'll see it, and Dad will think we're not lying about being at the quarry."

It was a good cover story, so that's what we decided to do.

Before we left for the woods, both my friends pestered me to tell them what my dad had said about why people didn't like their children playing near the quarry pool. I told them the whole story. All about the boy and how he was my dad's friend, and how he saved his life and that I was named him after him.

"What about the two boys who drowned 30 years earlier?" Thomas asked, once I had finished.

"I need to speak to my grandma and grandad about it," I said. "They were their friends."

We went to the end of the garden, to Paul's dad's shed, and grabbed a long rope. The one we found was about four times longer than what we needed, but we took it all the same and started making our way down towards the woods.

The woods were situated between the old football field and the quarry; they were vast and unmanaged, and covered an area about the size of ten football fields. They were full of all types of trees, including lots of hundred-year-old oaks, which were ideal for making rope swings in, along with evergreen trees, which were great for making camps and hideouts around the base.

There was a stream flowing from the quarry through the centre of the woods and eventually into a river. It was about five feet wide when it passed through the woods, and great for splashing about in on hot days. The oak tree we chose to build the rope swing on was on the edge of the woods overlooking the water, with branches that spanned over the stream.

While we were getting ready to put up the swing I caught sight of Sean and David walking towards us. I never used to get on with them as they were a little bit older and didn't have much time for me, so we didn't really play much. Plus, they liked to get me into trouble.

However, on this occasion, seeing them was a stroke of luck because I knew they'd tell Dad that we were in the woods playing on the rope swing, which would help with our cunning cover story for getting down to the quarry without being found out.

When they reached us, Sean said, "Remember you owe us a favour?"

I rolled my eyes and said, "What is it?"

"We need you to cover for us. We're going down town to see some girls," David told me. "Something you wouldn't know anything about, little boy!"

"Down town?" I repeated. "If Dad finds out, he'll kill you."

Dad never liked any of us straying too far from the village.

"He won't find out!" Sean said smugly. "Because if he does, he'll find out about you going down the quarry yesterday and you'll be in way more trouble than us. Besides, no one ever drowned down town."

They both laughed and walked off. Even though I was only 10, I thought they were behaving a little callously, since it was Dad's friend who had died.

"Come on then, you two," I said to Thomas and Paul, who had stopped what they were doing to watch the conversation between my brothers and me. "Let's make this rope swing, then."

We got to work.

"I'll climb the tree," I decided. "Thomas, you can throw the rope up."

So, off I went and climbed the tree. It was about 40 feet tall, but I scrambled up it as if it was only five feet. I loved climbing trees, particularly ones that seemed too hard or impossible for others to climb, and I was always pushing myself further than I should. If my parents could have seen how high up I was, I would probably have been grounded for the rest of the summer holidays.

Thomas threw the rope up as hard as he could, but it took three attempts before I caught it.

"Third time's a charm!" I shouted and laughed.

I tied it off on the thickest branch I could find that hung over the bank, so that we could swing right out over the stream and possibly end our swing with an undignified dunk in the water if we weren't careful.

After I climbed back down, Paul said, "We'd best test it and play with it for a little while before we go down the quarry."

"Okay," we all agreed.

We all took turns. Each one of us would swing out further and wider to try and beat the others.

We were having quite a good morning, considering we'd only built the swing as a cover story to get down to the quarry without adult interference, but we'd had a great deal of fun swinging back and forth and whooping when one of us fell into the stream. In the end, we spent the whole morning there.

As the day drew on, my stomach began to rumble, so I said, "It's time to go home for lunch, but when we come back out shall we go down the water?"

Thomas and Paul both agreed, so we raced back home to get something to eat, and to appease our mothers.

After lunch we all went down the quarry as planned. When we got there we found some plastic bottles that we'd stashed in the bushes earlier that week.

We put some stones in them and put the lids back on, so that when we threw them in the water they would float half-in and half-out of it. This made it difficult to hit them, but they would float around for hours and we had great fun trying to sink them.

After a while, I heard something. "Shush," I said. "I think I just heard someone shout."

"Paul, be quiet, it could be our parents!" Thomas hissed.

We all listened, but all we could hear was the wind blowing through the trees - then it went quiet. The same deathly quiet I had experienced that morning.

Across the water came the sound of girls singing: "Ring a ring o' roses, a pocketful of posies, a-tishoo, a-tishoo, we all fall down!"

Excited, I looked around, but I couldn't see them; nor could I hear Thomas or Paul behind me.

"Can you hear that?" I asked them without turning around. "Can you hear the girls singing?"

They didn't answer me, so I turned around to find they were gone! "Paul, Thomas where are you?" I shouted, frantically looking around.

There was no answer and I couldn't see them. I was so confused. Where had they gone? Why had they hidden from me? Although I didn't feel worried, or scared being down there on my own, I thought I'd better walk back towards home and look for them.

Just then, they both appeared as if from nowhere, over my shoulder.

"Where did you just go?" Thomas demanded. "One minute you were here and the next minute you'd hidden from us!"

"I didn't just disappear, I just went quiet to hear the girls singing across the water," I told him, surprised.

"What girls?" Paul asked.

"We didn't hear anything at all," said Thomas.

"They were!" I insisted. "They were singing and when I turned around to ask you if you could hear, you'd gone."

"Something weird's going on here and I don't like it," said Thomas, frowning. "I'm going home."

"Me too," Paul agreed.

"Well, I'm not staying down here on my own," I said, so we all set off towards the village.

As we walked together, we discussed what had just happened.

I explained, "I heard the same girls' voices singing the nursery rhyme like before, and when I turned around to ask if you heard them too, I couldn't see you."

Paul said, "That was about the same time you disappeared. We thought you'd hidden in the long grass for a joke. Where were you?"

"I could ask you the same question," I said, glancing at both of them along my shoulder.

"We never went anywhere!" Paul insisted. "You just disappeared, almost in front of our eyes."

"This is a little bit freaky," said Thomas.

"I know." I laughed as we carried on walking. "We've got to find out what's going on."

Nothing more was said about it after that, but each of us wondered whether the others were just playing a joke on us, or whether something mysterious really had happened.

"Are we going to go and play on the rope swing tomorrow?" I asked, as we neared our road.

"Yes," they both answered.

We all agreed to meet at 9 o'clock the next morning.

"But not too early though, George, I like my lie-ins," laughed Thomas.

Back home, I sat at the table with a smile on my face, still excited.

"What you are looking so happy about?" my mum asked.

"Nothing, just had a good day, thanks."

That night I couldn't sleep right away - my excitement just grew and grew - but eventually I did drift off.

The next morning, I woke up early again. It must've been 7 o'clock in the morning. I was so excited to get up and get out - not to play on the rope swing we'd built (even though that was pretty cool) - but to go back down to the quarry and uncover the mystery of the singing girls.

Chapter Three

The First Encounter

The next morning I got up, got dressed, and went downstairs.

"Morning, Mum," I said, as she passed me my breakfast.

"Morning, George, what are you up to today?" she asked.

"Just the rope swing," I replied as I wolfed my breakfast down. "Nothing too exciting."

Shortly afterwards, I went out, telling my mum I was going to call on my friends.

I didn't go straight to their houses, though. I wanted to go back to the quarry on my own to see if I could hear or see the girls again. I didn't want Thomas or Paul to come this time, as I wasn't completely sure if they'd believed me the day before.

When I got there, everything seemed normal. The breeze blowing, the water glistening in the morning sun, the birds singing - and absolutely no girls.

I sat down, laid back, and looked up at the sky.

After a few minutes, again, everything seemed to become silent before I began to hear the girls singing and laughing.

I sat up, thrilled. I could definitely hear them; it wasn't a dream! Once again, it sounded like they were across the water from where I was sitting. I stood up and this time, there they were: three girls - all about my age - playing across the water.

I looked over and even waved at them, but they didn't look back. I started throwing stones in the water at one of the bottles that was still there from the day before to see if they would notice, but still they didn't look over.

I threw a bigger stone to make a bigger splash to try and get their attention, which seemed to do the trick. Just then, one of the girls looked over and screamed as if I'd frightened her.

"Sorry!" she shouted, when she recovered. "I just got a fright when I saw you."

"That's okay," I shouted back. "I'm just here throwing stones at these plastic bottles in the water."

"What's plastic?" one of the girls asked, laughing.

I never gave it a thought.

"Are you coming over?" one of the girls shouted.

"Ok, I'll walk round!" I almost skipped around the pool, I was so excited to meet them.

I heard them laughing and playing still, but the further I walked around the quarry, the quieter the girls became. I looked back and I could still see them, but as I got to the other side of the water, they'd gone!

How rude, I thought to myself. *They asked me to come around and then they just go and hide.*

I didn't feel upset with them, not really. Just a little disappointed. I looked around for them a little while longer, but there was no evidence of their presence. They were nowhere to be seen.

Time was pressing on, so I decided to go and meet up with my friends as planned.

As I walked back around to make my way home, I heard one of the girls shout: "I thought you were coming over!"

"I did," I replied, pleased to see them again. "But I couldn't find you."

"No, you didn't!" she shouted back. "You just went."

I thought, *that's weird. Like when Paul and Thomas vanished before.*

"I have to go now," I shouted across the water. "Maybe we'll see you later?"

"Maybe!" one of them shouted back.

I went to call on Thomas and Paul.

When all three of us were together, I said, "Let's go down to the rope swing, I need to tell you about this morning," and off we went.

On the way, I told them about how I'd gone to the quarry first thing that morning.

"Why?" Paul asked, shocked. "Why would you go down there on your own?"

"I wanted to see if I could see the girls I heard singing yesterday," I replied.

"And did you see them?" he asked.

"Yes, and I spoke to them."

"Who are they, then?" Thomas asked.

"I don't know!" I said. "When I went around to meet up with them they'd run off, then when I came back to go home I saw them again! I think they were either playing a game or something strange is happening at the quarry, like when you saw me disappear yesterday!"

"We can go down and try to meet them now, if you like," Thomas suggested.

"Okay," I said excitedly.

"Come on then, let's go and find these girls," Thomas declared, and so we set off to the quarry.

"Where were these girls, then?" Paul asked, when we arrived at the water's edge.

"They were over there, singing when I saw them," I explained, pointing out the spot.

"How did you talk to them?" Paul asked.

"I was just shouting across the water."

"Well, I can't see anything now," he said.

"Me either," said Thomas.

Paul said, "Let's throw stones at the bottles while we wait to see if they turn up."

It wasn't long after we started throwing stones when it went quiet. By this point I'd learnt that the wind always stopped just before I saw them. Sure enough, a few seconds later I heard them shouting, laughing and having fun.

"There they are!" I cried. "I can see them playing across the water."

"I can't see them!" Paul said.

"Or hear them," Thomas added. Then he frowned. "No! Wait a minute, I hear them now!"

"Me too!" Paul shouted, excited.

"Over there, I can see them - all three of them," I said, pointing over the water.

"We can only hear them," Thomas said, exchanging a puzzled, wide-eyed glance with Paul.

"Keep looking over there," I whispered, as we moved closer to them. "They're over there in the long grass - clear as day."

"Yes, I see them now!" Thomas hissed, excited.

"Yes!" Paul agreed. "It's like they just appeared from nowhere."

"Hi, girls!" I shouted over.

"Co-eee!" Thomas yelled.

"Co-eee?" Paul turned to look at Thomas and burst out laughing.

"I'm trying to get their attention," he replied and laughed too.

"I don't think they can see us," I said.

Just then, one of the girls looked over and shouted to us, "Hello! Are you coming over?"

"Yes!" I shouted back as we started walking around towards where they were playing.

All three of us were excited to be able to see the girls and we walked quickly over the high area where the wall had a drop into the water of over six feet in order to show off. That part of the wall was narrow, so waling across that point was a little risky and dangerous. I suppose we were hoping they would think we were brave.

Just then, while we were walking around the bank, Paul and Thomas went quiet; I turned around and they'd gone. I shouted their names, but they didn't answer. The girls, however, were exactly where they should have been.

"Where did your friends go?" one of them asked.

"I think they've run off," I said, though I suspected it had more to do with the weird haze over the water.

"Maybe they are shy," she replied.

"Maybe," I said. "Maybe."

I introduced myself to the girls. "Hi! My name is George."

"My name is Aly," said the girl who'd been speaking to me. "And this is Em and Iris."

All three girls smiled at me.

"Where are you from?" I said.

"We live in the village," Aly replied.

"I live in the village, too," I told them.

"Have you just moved there?" Em asked.

"No, I've been there for years," I said, surprised. "Why?"

They all looked at one another as if I was lying, but said no more about it.

"Who are the other two boys and why didn't they come over?" Aly asked.

"Thomas and Paul," I said. "My best friends. I'm not sure why they didn't come around. I'd better go looking for them."

As I walked back over to the other side of the quarry pool I heard Paul and Thomas both shouting my name.

"George!"

"George!"

Thomas spotted me. "Where have you been? One second you were here and the next you and the girls had gone."

"Yeah," said Paul, "we've been shouting you."

"I went over to see them and you never came," I told them. "Just wait there a minute, while I go over and say goodbye to the girls."

I jogged back around to where the girls were playing, and as I got to them I turned around and saw that Paul and Thomas had gone again.

"I'm going to have to go home and look for my friends," I told Aly, thinking this would be the simplest explanation. "If I get found down here on my own I'll get into real trouble with my parents."

"Why?" Iris asked.

"Apparently three boys drowned here a few years ago, so my dad says I'm not allowed to play here," I explained.

"We've never heard of anyone drowning in the quarry," Em said, sharing worried glances with her friends.

Maybe it's not common knowledge, I thought to myself.

Aloud, I said, "I don't know. It's just what my dad said. I'd better go home anyway."

"Alright," Iris said.

"Are you coming back soon?" Aly asked.

"Maybe tomorrow," I said.

They waved goodbye and I set off back towards where I'd left my friends. Just as I reached the patch of long grass where I'd last seen Thomas and Paul, I saw them reappear as if from nowhere. All three of us jumped and had a fright. It was so spooky, seeing them appear out of thin air like that.

"Something's going on," Thomas said excitedly. "When you walked over there, we saw you and the girls disappear through a haze!"

"Something really weird is happening," Paul agreed. "We need to find out why and how you're able to disappear and reappear - and where you go!"

"I know, something very strange is going on here," I said. "What do you think it is?"

"I don't know, but it's really cool," said Paul, who was obviously just as curious and excited as I was.

"Let's go down the rope swing and talk about it," I suggested, so we did.

We didn't talk much on our way down. We were busy listening out for anyone who might spot us leaving the area of the quarry and get us into trouble. When we reached the swing, though, the discussion started in earnest. Thomas and Paul wanted to know everything they could about the girls, what it felt like when the haze came down around me and so on. All three of us wanted to know what was going on, and how it all - whatever it was - worked.

There were so many unanswered questions, so we decided to start with the ones we actually knew something about.

"Where did the girls say they were from?" Paul asked, taking his turn on the swing.

"They said they lived in the village," I told him.

"Where in the village?" Thomas asked.

"I didn't ask," I admitted. "But I told them I lived in the village too, and they asked if I'd just moved here."

"Very strange," Paul said ponderously. "Very strange."

Like private detectives, we started to work out how we could find out who these girls were, where they lived, and why they kept appearing and disappearing. We couldn't wait to get our teeth into this new adventure.

As the day drew on we had to go home, but we agreed to meet up early the next morning.

Nobody will be sleeping in tomorrow, I thought.

All three of us wanted to spend the whole day on this new investigation. It was thrilling, to think we were discovering something magical. We were certain the girls were involved, somehow. I could only hope that my brothers didn't put a spanner in the works by wanting to come to the quarry with me. I hoped they would choose to go into town again.

I sat down and watched TV for a little while, but my head wasn't really in it - it was still across the quarry with our strange new friends - so as the evening drew on I went off to bed, excited and ready for the next day.

Chapter Four

Discovering the Magic Door

The next morning, I got up out of bed with a spring in my step, excited for the day ahead. I couldn't wait to find out all I could about the three girls; I couldn't wait to join my two best friends in becoming the best detectives the village had ever seen.

"Good morning, Mum!" I said, as I skipped through the living room.

"Someone's in a good mood today," she observed. "What would you like for breakfast?"

"I might just go without breakfast this morning, Mum!"

"Oh no you won't. A growing boy needs his breakfast," she admonished.

"Okay then," I said, thinking of something quick to make and eat, "jam on toast, then, please."

Even so, it seemed to take an age before it was ready. I was so eager to get outside and start figuring things out that I was practically dancing around on the kitchen chair.

As she brought my breakfast through she asked, "What are you up to today?"

"We're going down to play on the rope swing again."

"Are you playing with your brothers today?" she asked.

I shrugged. I hoped not. "I don't know, depends what they're doing."

I was beginning to feel a bit guilty about lying to my mum about where I was - and where my brothers had been. It turns out, being a master detective sometimes requires a little deceit.

I called on Thomas first. I had barely knocked on the door when it opened.

"You ready?" I asked.

He was still doing up his shoelace, but he hopped out of the door all the same. "Yes, let's go and get Paul."

As we walked towards his house our friend was already closing his front door. We beamed at one another. This was going be an adventure of a lifetime, we just knew it.

Off we went, straight to the quarry, discussing what we were going to do as we went.

"We should sneak up among the long grass to see if we can hear them," Thomas suggested.

"No, that's a stupid idea," I told him. "The girls already know who I am. We just want to try and find out why they keep appearing out of nowhere."

"Well, we only ever seem to hear them when we're on this side of the water," reasoned Paul. "Let's sit here and wait."

"Now what?" Thomas asked, when we were lounging on the grass. He was probably still a bit miffed that I'd called his idea 'stupid'.

"Well, normally I hear the girls singing, the wind stops, and it goes quiet," I told them. "So, I suppose we wait for that."

So we sat back and watched the clouds rolling lazily across the summer sky.

"I love those big, white, fluffy clouds," Thomas said, after a while.

"I know, me too," I replied.

"What do you think clouds are made of?" Paul asked.

"Water, I think," I said, though it seemed silly if I thought too much about it. They didn't look particularly watery. "Just water."

"Could they stay up there like that if they were made of water?" Thomas asked, sceptical.

"I don't know," I said. "They must do, somehow, but when they get too heavy, that's when it rains."

This, naturally, led into quite a deep debate about clouds and water, and just when we'd got onto talking about how the wind worked, everything went quiet - almost as if it had heard us.

"This is it," I said breathlessly, sitting up. "This is what happens! The wind seems to stop and the birds go quiet."

Sure enough, as soon as I finished speaking, the sound of the girls' laughter and singing drifted across the water.

"Do you hear that?" I asked.

"Yes!" they both replied at once, tripping over one another with excitement.

All three of us looked across the water, where we could see the girls running around and playing.

"Why were they not there a minute ago?" Paul asked.

"I don't know," I said. I had been thinking about this a lot. "This is why I think they've got a hideout nearby, or maybe they do just appear from nowhere."

As I said it, a cold shiver travelled down the back of each of our spines. It was as if they were ghosts. It was all so spooky!

"I'm a little bit scared," Thomas admitted.

"There's no reason to be scared," I told him. "They're still only three girls."

At this point, the one who'd introduced herself as Aly spotted us and shouted over, "Hello! Are you coming over?"

"Yes!" we all called back at the same time.

As we all made our way around the quarry again we walked over the wall, as we had the day before. When I reached a particular point along the wall, Thomas and Paul disappeared.

Shocked, but not entirely surprised given the events of the last couple of days, I stopped dead in my tracks. Quickly, I retraced my steps and walked backwards along the wall. About five paces back, both Paul and Thomas reappeared, their faces as white as chalk.

"It happened again," said Thomas, gulping in fear. "You were walking in front of us - just like yesterday - and as if by magic you just disappeared through a shimmer of light, like a heat haze."

"That must be about the same time I heard you stop talking," I said. "Something's going on right here, when I pass this area of grass," I added, pointing to the bank beside me. "It seems like only I can get through, or across - or wherever it is I go."

"How are we going to do this, then?" Paul asked, frowning at the patch of grass. "We need to come up with a plan so that when you go through, we all follow you."

"Why don't we all hold hands?" Thomas suggested.

"I'm not holding your hand," Paul refused, laughing.

"He might be right, though, Paul," I argued. "At some point, I disappear. Let's all hold hands - but we won't tell anyone!" I added and we all laughed.

None of us really wanted to hold each other's hands, really, so we took one another by the wrist instead.

"Here," said Thomas. "This is where we see you disappear."

Together, we took a step over the threshold of whatever it was that could make me and three girls appear and disappear. Fortunately, holding onto each other seemed to have worked. Releasing one another's wrists, we carried on towards the girls.

Thomas and Paul were looking around at their surroundings.

"It all looks a little bit strange over this side, don't you think?" Paul asked. "I mean, different to what it is when you look across the water, almost like the trees aren't as big or the grass as long."

"This is seriously weird," Thomas seconded.

I nodded, but we had nearly reached the girls.

Aly beckoned us, calling, "Are you coming, or not?"

We ran over to meet them.

"Hello Aly, Em, Iris," I said, introducing my friends. "This is Thomas and Paul."

They all said hello to one another.

"Where are you from?" Iris asked.

"From the village," Paul said.

"Did you just move here too, with George?" Em asked.

"No, we've all lived here for years," Paul said, but they didn't believe him and thought we were just joking with them.

Aly asked, "Do you want to play a game?"

"Yes," Paul replied. "How about hide and seek?"

"Alright then, let's play hide and seek, girls against boys."

"Okay, you three turn around and count to a hundred, and we'll go and hide," Aly said, and everyone agreed.

So, we counted to one hundred with our eyes closed. We could hear the girls laughing and giggling as they ran off.

"This is going to be easy," I said, still with my eyes shut.

"Still, let's split up, just in case they have got a hideout," said Paul, beginning to run. Paul and Thomas went off in one direction; I went off in the other.

I followed the sounds of the girls giggling.

This is going to be a little too *easy!* I thought.

I put my head over a bush and grinned. "Found you! I've found them!" I shouted to Thomas and Paul. There was no response, so I shouted again. "They're here!" The girls stood up together, giggling.

"That didn't take long," Em remarked.

"I know," I said proudly.

"Where are your friends?" Aly asked.

"I don't know," I replied. "I think they went off in a different direction."

"Well they didn't come past us, or we'd have seen them," said Iris.

Aly looked around. "Maybe they've gone in the woods looking for you."

The girls were excited to find them, thinking it was part of the game, but I had a sneaking suspicion that they were on the other side of the quarry, unable to see us.

After around about 10 minutes of looking for them, the girls gave up.

"They must have gone home - some friends they are," Em said, shaking her head.

"Maybe they needed to use the toilet, or something," I suggested.

"Maybe," Aly replied.

"I'd better go and find them," I said.

As I said goodbye I walked off around the quarry. More than halfway around, I saw Thomas and Paul.

"What happened?" I asked.

Thomas explained, "The same thing as yesterday. As we walked back to this side of the quarry we couldn't see or hear you, or the girls. Are we still playing?"

I looked at him. "No, you've been gone ages."

"No we haven't," he protested. "We can't have been here more than three minutes."

"Three minutes?" I asked, mouth agape.

"Yes," Paul agreed, looking at me oddly. "We only started playing the game a minute ago!"

"That's very strange," I said. "I've been looking for you for the last 10 minutes!"

Thomas shook his head. "We came here to wait for you because we knew this is where you'd turn up."

"Then it must be this stretch of land here that does something odd," I said, thinking aloud. "Between this side of the quarry and the other, only I can travel back and forth to wherever the girls are, but it seems that when I leave you both you're stuck in time. What was 10 or 15 minutes for me, was just a few minutes for you."

"Where is it that you think we're going?" Paul asked.

"I don't know," Thomas replied. "Maybe we're going to another dimension!"

"Another dimension?" Paul repeated. "What on Earth's that?"

Thomas went on to say that he remembered watching a film with his dad about a man who went from one dimension to another. "It's like a parallel universe," he said, when he was finished.

"What is a parallel universe?" I asked Thomas.

"I'm not *really* sure," he said, with a frown, "but I think it's when there are two worlds that are next to each other that are almost the same, but not, and you're able to pass from one world to another."

"Then why can George go through on his own, but we must go with him?" Paul asked.

"I don't know."

"George, have you got any ideas?" Paul asked, as we kicked stones on the bank of the quarry.

"Well only one," I replied. "When I came down to the quarry the other day on my own - the first morning I heard the girls singing - I was lying on the grass when I heard a large bang and a huge gust of wind blew across me and I'm not sure, but it felt a lot like I might have got an electric shock."

"Wow," said Paul. "So, if we'd got up earlier that day, all three of us would be able to travel!"

"Maybe it had something to do with the Northern Lights the other night?" said Thomas.

"Yeah," I agreed. "Maybe something in that explosion gave me the ability to go from one side to another - but to where?"

"I don't know," said Thomas, grinning, "but it's very cool."

"Yeah, it's like magic or something," Paul agreed, excited.

"What should we call this area where we go through?" I said. "We can't just keep calling it 'the patch of grass'."

After a little while, having come up with various ridiculous and funny names, we eventually settled on the 'magic door'.

"Okay," I said. "It's very important that we don't tell anyone about this."

"Yes," said Paul. "If our parents find out, we'll be in so much trouble."

"Besides," Thomas added, "I don't want anyone else finding out about our secret door."

We set off for home, excited and talking about the new magic door. We agreed to meet the next day, but this time with a plan: we had to find a way to find out what was going on - find out who can see us and find out where we were going.

CHAPTER FIVE

WHO'S WHO?

The next day, the three of us were playing on the rope swing - which had become part of our morning routine, now - discussing how we should use this new magic door.

Paul said, "I'm absolutely gutted that I have to go on holiday next week."

He was going to Spain for a week with his family. Up until we'd found the magic door at the quarry, he'd been quite looking forward to it.

"I mean, it's awesome that you're going on holiday, but I'd be absolutely gutted too," I admitted. "Here we are, just about to start an adventure of a lifetime, and you have to leave."

"We'll tell you all about it when you get back," Thomas offered.

Paul scowled at us both, but there was little malice in it, and I laughed.

Taking turns to swing out over the stream (we were getting very good at it now, with all the practice we were having), we decided that we'd have to stay close to one another on the other side of the door. Since I was apparently the only one who could travel through it - a fact

I felt extremely proud of - none of us wanted either of the other two getting stuck there if we got separated. They seemed to be able to get back themselves, so as long as we could get back to the quarry, we figured we would probably be okay.

We also needed to find out what the time difference was between what Thomas was insisting on calling the 'parallel universe'.

"Paul, do you have a watch?" I asked, as we waited for Thomas to pick himself up out of the stream after an unsuccessful swing.

"No, but my dad has one in his drawer that he doesn't use." He pulled a face. "We could probably borrow it, but we must put it back as soon as we're finished, or I'll be in deep trouble."

"Good," I said. "We're going to need another one as well." Then, on their looks of confusion, I explained, "If there is a time difference between one side of the magic door and another, the best way to find out what that difference is would be by setting both watches to exactly the same time, then I travel through the magic door with one watch and stay there for exactly one hour. Or half an hour. Something."

"I don't follow you," Paul said, as I took my turn on the swing.

As I swung back and forth, I heard Thomas telling Paul, "I think what he means is when he comes back, his watch will be faster than ours and we'll then know how long he's been there, compared to how long we've seen him disappear for. Is that what you mean, George?"

"Yes, exactly that," I replied, swinging off again.

"Well, we need to find another watch, then," said Thomas. "I don't have one."

"I know, I'll ask my grandad," I said.

My grandparents were pretty good like that; they never asked questions about where I was going, or what I was up to - though they did seem interested in if I was enjoying myself - and best of all, they never hassled me about going down the quarry.

"I'm sure he has one," I said, thinking back. "I've seen him wearing it in the past, but he doesn't wear it anymore, so maybe he'll lend us it."

This was why instead of going straight down to the quarry, we decided to go back into the village and grab the watches.

On the way to Paul's house, Thomas's mum shouted out of an upstairs window, "Thomas, you need to take the dog out for his walk!"

Thomas rolled his eyes. "Yes, Mum!" he shouted back as he grabbed the dog.

On we went to Paul's house. Thomas and I played outside with the dog while we waited. About 10 minutes later he emerged with his father's watch, which was digital and made of black plastic.

"Great," I said, as Thomas examined it. "Now we just need to get the other watch from my grandad, and we're all set."

As we got to my grandparents' house I asked, "Are you two coming in?"

"No, we'll just wait here," Thomas said. "I couldn't take the dog into your grandad's house, anyway. It's rude."

"No, my grandad likes dogs," I said. "I'm sure he won't mind you bringing him in."

"Alright," said Thomas. "If he likes dogs, then it might help butter him up for when you ask to borrow his watch."

Just as I was about to knock, the door opened: it was Grandad.

"I thought I heard voices out here! Here comes trouble!" he shouted to Grandma. "George is here." He laughed. "Hello Thomas, hello Paul. And who is this?"

Grandad bent down to stroke the dog, making a huge fuss of him. Patch loved having a fuss, so he got excited and lay on his back to have his head rubbed.

"What brings you around here on this beautiful morning?" Grandad asked, still stroking Patch. "Why aren't you playing down in the woods?"

"Nothing," I said. "I just wanted to come around and see my favourite grandma and grandad."

Grandad gave me a very knowing look and grinned. "What do you want?"

"Me and my friends want to try a little experiment and we need a watch for it," I explained, confident that he would want to help us.

Straightaway, without question, Grandad put his hand in his pocket, pulled out a watch, and passed it over to me.

"You can take this watch but be very careful with it. It was given to me by my best friend," he told me, setting the time and winding it up for me.

"There you go."

Grandad had been so generous with lending us his watch, and I felt that I needed to stay there for a little bit longer, or I'd have seemed ungrateful. I also wanted to get away so we could get back to the quarry, but without any awkward silence, Grandad said, "Off you go then, go and play. Have fun."

I think he knew how eager I was to be off.

I smiled at him and said, "I will, thanks again for the watch. I promise I'll take good care of it."

With our borrowed treasure, we hurried back towards the quarry, Patch running happily alongside us.

At the door, I said, "Thomas, you'll have to wait here with Patch, while I go through the magic door."

He nodded. "I'll let him have a run around."

"What are you doing, Paul?" I asked. "Are you coming with me, or staying here?"

He volunteered to stay with Thomas and keep an eye out. I think he was still a little bit nervous and didn't really want to come through with me, as the reality of what was really happening was starting to hit us - especially with this experiment.

"Okay, let's look at the time."

It was 10:55 a.m.

"Let's wait until exactly 11 o'clock and then I'll travel through the magic door," I said. "I'll wait there exactly half an hour according to my watch and then come back."

"Yes."

"Yep."

We were all agreed, so for the next five minutes we talked excitedly about how we would probably be the first people ever to travel from one universe to another.

It was the most thrilling yet nerve-racking thing we'd ever done, and probably the most dangerous thing we would ever do, but given the age we were, it felt like a thing that had to be done.

"It's nearly 11 o'clock, George," Thomas said, checking Paul's dad's watch.

"Okay, I'll go and stand at the magic door. On the turn of 11, I'll walk through."

Tentatively, I walked up to the magic door, getting as close as I could without actually going through it. I put the watch on my wrist and looked back at Thomas and Paul, who both nodded solemnly. For a moment, I wondered whether I would ever see them again, but just then it turned 11 o'clock and I started walking forward. I could hear Patch going absolutely mad behind me, barking and whining, as if he knew something was up. Abruptly, the dog's barking disappeared and I could no longer hear them.

I looked around the quarry and couldn't see anyone at all - not even the girls.

I settled down to wait, watching the time carefully, then from the woods behind me Aly and Em sneaked up and pounced on me.

"Boo!" they shouted.

Already nervous and on edge, I nearly jumped out of my skin. "Cor!" I said. "You've just given me the fright of my life!"

The girls howled with laughter.

"You should have seen your face!" Em cried, giggling.

"Where did you just spring up from?" Aly asked.

"I just walked over from the village," I lied, counting on the fact that they'd just come out of the woods.

"That's a nice watch you're wearing," Em said, noticing it.

"Yes, I borrowed it from my grandad."

"Why do you need a watch?" Aly asked.

"No real reason, it's just my mum said I must go home in half an hour and I'm not to be late."

I thought this was a good enough excuse to stop them asking questions.

I bit my lip. It occurred to me that when it came time for me to cross back through the door they would see me disappear, which would give them a fright - and I would never be able to explain myself.

Luckily, Aly said, "We're going to the village ourselves to meet Iris and then we're going down into town for our mum. Do you want to walk up with us?"

"No," I said sharply. I didn't want anyone else to see me just yet - and the experiment would be ruined if I didn't stick to it. "I'm tired. I'm going to lie here for 10 minutes and have a sleep."

"Alright," Em laughed. "Suit yourself, *Grandad*."

"I'll probably see you tomorrow if you're down here?" I said. It wasn't as if I didn't want to play with them, there was just more going on than they knew about.

"Alright," Aly said. "I look forward to it!"

And off they went, holding hands and skipping.

Wow, I thought to myself, checking the watch. *That was close*!

There were only two minutes left before I was supposed to go back through. I went and stood as close to the magic door as I could and on the turn of 11:30 I walked through.

As I walked through, I heard the dog going absolutely mad and barking, finding Paul and Thomas looking at me and holding the dog back.

"Hi! How long were you there?" Thomas asked. "Patch, calm down. It's only George."

"Exactly half an hour," I replied. "What time is it now?"

Paul looked at his watch and said, "You've been gone exactly 10 minutes."

We put both watches together and he was right: Paul's watch said 11:10 and mine said 11:30. We were all so excited.

"Do you know what this means?" I gasped. "It means I've travelled in time, or something like that."

Thomas said, "No, it's just the other universe is moving faster, so for every hour here in our dimension it's three hours in the girls' dimension."

"Yes, I think you're right, Thomas," said Paul. "Their time must go three times faster than ours."

"I also saw Aly and Em when I was there," I told them.

"What about Iris?" Thomas asked.

"No, Thomas. Sorry, Iris wasn't there. She was back in the village." I laughed. "I'm only asking, but do you fancy her?"

He immediately went red in the face.

"I don't fancy her, I just like her."

"This is so amazing!" I said, as he scowled. "We could actually extend the amount of time we play out - and our school holidays - if we keep travelling through the magic door."

"I know," Thomas said. "We should also make a map!"

"A map!" Paul echoed.

"Yes, like a treasure map, but with our magic door on it."

"We could do that, but it would be important that nobody could find the map," I warned.

"Why?" Thomas reasoned. "Without you nobody would be able to go through the magic door. They'd think we were only pretending."

"Yes, you're right," I said, realising what he said was true. "I'm the one with the magic powers."

They both laughed.

"Magic powers?" Paul grinned. "You were just lucky you were hit by that shockwave, that's all."

"Even so," I said, "I'm the one who can travel backwards and forwards, so I am the door keeper!"

We all just burst out laughing at this.

"This is going to be real fun," said Paul, beaming from ear to ear.

"We need to take the dog back now," Thomas said.

Patch had calmed down a bit by this point. I think he was just confused to see me disappear and reappear, but then he might also have been able to sense the door.

As we were walking up towards Thomas's house, Paul said we needed to get some paper and some pencils and a lighter.

"Why a lighter?" Thomas asked.

"Because we need to draw the map, then we need to scorch the edges of the paper to make it look like a real treasure map," he said.

"Well, I can get the pencil and paper," Thomas said, "but there's no way I can get my hands on a lighter."

"That's okay," I said. "I'll tell my mum I'm getting a drink, sneak upstairs, and steal - I mean, borrow - one of my mum's lighters."

Thomas nodded, then went into his house to let Patch have a drink and go to sleep after his walk, and to get some pencils and paper. Meanwhile, Paul and I went over to my house for a drink.

We went in and while I was 'borrowing' the lighter, Paul kept my mum and dad talking and distracted.

"Got it," I said to him in an undertone when I got back downstairs. "I'm off out now," I told my parents, who gave me the usual warnings about being careful.

Thomas was waiting for us at the end of the road.

"Let's go down to the rope swing and we can start drawing up the map!" he said.

So, off we went down to the woods, talking about what we were going to put on the map. It was so exciting, like we were having a proper adventure.

Between us, we decided what we were going to draw on the map. Paul had the best drawing skills so we let him draw it. We named the map 'Treasure Map', so if anyone ever found it they wouldn't know it was the magic door. We put an X where the magic door was and wrote underneath "treasure".

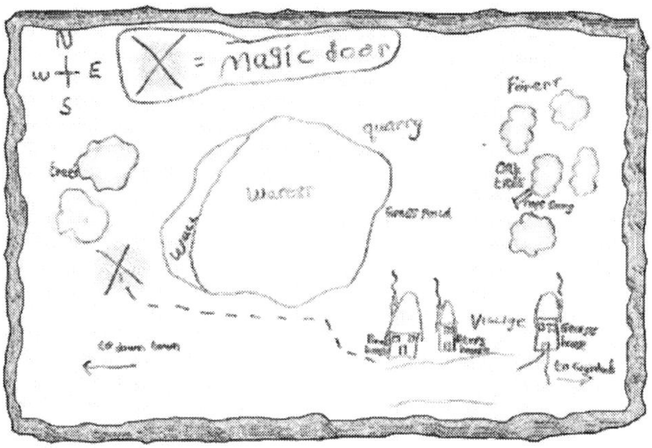

In the map was drawn the village, the quarry, the woods, and a dotted line from the village all the way to the X.

"Okay, how are we going to burn the edges?" Paul asked.

I said, "Roll it up into a tube, then get the lighter and run it up and down the length of it, and on the edges."

So, Thomas rolled it up into a tube and I started to burn the edges, but almost straightaway the whole map burst into flames and he quickly dropped it. It landed in the dry grass at our feet, which also started to catch fire. Quickly, we stamped the flames out.

"That was close!" I said, when the fire was out and we'd had the chance to calm down a little. "We could have burned the woods down! And we've destroyed the map."

"We need to come up with a better plan," said Thomas, drawing the map out again while we thought about it.

I suggested that we dampen the map with a little bit of water, so it wasn't as easy to burn.

"That's a good idea," Thomas said.

We knelt by the stream (next to the rope swing) that was fed from the quarry. I put my hand in the water and used the water to moisten the map.

"Let's try again," I said. "This time, you can hold the lighter, then if it goes up in flames it's your fault." I laughed.

Thomas started burning the edges.

"That did the trick," Paul said. "It's burning the edges and this time we're not likely to burn down the woods!"

We all laughed, partly from relief.

"Where should we put the map to keep it safe?" I asked.

"I've got an idea," Thomas said. "Why don't we bury it?"

"Okay," Paul and I agreed.

"But where?" Paul asked.

We looked around the woods and decided that we'd bury it next to the largest oak tree, where we'd always be able to find it again.

"We can't put it in the ground like this or it will be ruined," I said.

"I know!" Paul said. "I have a thick cardboard tube at home with plastic caps on either end. I'll get it out tonight and we can bury it tomorrow."

"Good idea," said Thomas, gathering up his pencils and paper.

"I can't wait to go through the magic door tomorrow," I said.

"If we go through in the morning and stay there all day, we could still be back here for around lunchtime," Thomas worked out happily.

"Yes," Paul said, "but what if we're wrong about the time difference? What if we go back across the magic door, spend all day there, and realise that we've gone missing all day here?"

"He's right," Thomas said. "Everyone will be looking for us."

"You two just worry too much," I complained.

"It's okay for you," grumbled Thomas. "You can come and go as you please. If we want to come back and you don't, we're stuck."

I was horrified. "I would never leave you there and I'd never ever come back without you."

"We should make a pact on that," Paul suggested.

So, we pressed our hands into a circle and said, in unison, "We promise to never ever leave another on the other side of the magic door." Then we counted to three and threw our hands up in the air, laughing.

We decided that we'd go through the magic door for an hour this time, and leave Paul's watch somewhere nearby so we could collect it on the way back - and see if our theory about the time difference was correct.

"Now, where can we hide Paul's watch?" I asked.

"Yes," Paul said, looking worried. "If someone comes past and sees it they'll take it. And I'll get killed if my dad finds out I've lost it."

"Why don't we dig a hole under that rock over there?" Thomas suggested, pointing to a prominent rock near to the magic door.

"Okay, that makes sense," Paul agreed.

It was getting close to 5 o'clock, so we decided we would go through the door for a little while. We buried Paul's watch under the rock and stood by the magic door. This time, we didn't complain about holding hands at all. We were worried about someone being left behind, so we clung onto each other tightly.

"On the count of three," I said. "Three... two... one..."

We all walked forward together and the world changed around us. The trees were smaller, the grass longer, and the smell in the air was different. I hadn't noticed it before, but this time I did. In this place the air seemed a little bit fresher, but at the same time smoky, like a wood fire was burning somewhere nearby.

The girls weren't around this time. We could neither hear nor see them.

"We should explore a little bit," I said.

"Yes," Thomas replied.

"We all need to stay really close," Paul said. "We don't want to lose each other or slip back through the magic door."

Since we weren't sure how wide the door was, we stayed away from it altogether.

"Yeah, could you imagine being lost in another dimension, not being able to get home?" Thomas asked.

"Don't even say that, Thomas," I said. "That would be really bad. What would I tell your mum and dad?"

Carefully and slowly, we started walking around the quarry to areas we'd not been to before. We walked down towards the stream that ran through the woods.

"So far so good," I said. "How far do you want to go?"

"This is enough for now," Paul said. "I'm a little scared."

I was a little scared, too, but I didn't want to tell anyone; I wanted to act brave. I felt like the important one in the group because I was the only one who could unlock the magic door, but I fully understood why Thomas and Paul were more nervous than me.

We agreed to go back closer to the magic door and throw stones into the quarry pool, like we usually did, until the three hours had passed and we could go through.

"I wonder if the girls will come down," Thomas mused.

I pulled a face. "I hope not."

"Why?" Paul asked, seeming disappointed.

I said, "Think about it! We need to go back across the magic door at exactly 8 o'clock according to my watch, and if the girls come down and want to play, or want to go somewhere with us, how are we going to get back to the magic door - or even get through it without them seeing us disappear?"

"That's actually good thinking," said Paul. "I never thought of that."

"Me neither," Thomas said.

"I only thought of it because earlier on, when I saw Aly and Em, I was faced with the same problem."

As it grew closer to the time we needed to head back, we all walked over towards the magic door and linked our arms tightly together.

"Three... two... one," I said, then we all stepped forward.

We knew that we were back in our dimension at once. We recognised the trees and the lack of smoky air.

Quickly, we went over to the rock, rolled it over, and pulled out Paul's watch.

"What time is it, Paul?" I asked.

"It's 6 o'clock," he replied.

"That proves it, then," I said. We've been over there for three hours and only one hour has passed here."

"Wait a minute, then," Thomas said, thinking. "So, if we went there for one day we would age by one day, right? So when we come back, will we look one day older?"

"Well, yes," I said. "But how old can you get in one day?"

"Just saying," he said jokingly. "If we stayed there for one year, when we came back we would be older than Sean!"

I smiled and laughed. "That would be fun! I'd be his big brother and I'd be able to boss him around instead! Anyway, that's never going to happen. We can only ever go for the day, which means only a few hours will pass here."

We all agreed on these new rules: we stick together, we only go there for 12 hours or less - which would be four hours in our world - and we must stick to the rules whatever happened.

"A deal," I said.

We all put our hands in the middle of the circle and said, "Follow the rules," in unison, throwing our hands up in the air. "Deal," we all said, together.

"What are we going to do about the clothes they wear and the clothes we wear?" Thomas said.

"What do you mean?" I asked.

Paul replied, "He's right. The girls dress so differently to the girls in our world, so I'm guessing the boys do, too. We need to try and make our clothes look more like theirs."

So, we came up with the idea to go to the charity shop in town, where they had all sorts of old clothes.

"I can't afford to buy clothes, though," I said, with a grimace. "Not even from a charity shop. I don't get pocket money."

"You and me both," Thomas replied.

"I'll borrow five pounds out of my mum's purse," Paul said. "She'll never notice it's missing."

Things were getting serious now. We were committed to being explorers of another world.

"If we go now and I can grab the money, we can go to the shop today," he said. "It doesn't close until eight, but we'll have to sneak there and back, so our parents don't see us."

"Where will we keep the clothes?" I asked.

"We'll have to get a box!" replied Thomas. "A wooden box - and hide it in the bushes at the quarry, where no one can find it. Then, when we go through the door we can get changed."

"My grandad has some old wooden boxes in his shed; I could ask him if we could have one," I said.

Soon we were off with Paul's stolen (no, borrowed) five pounds to the local charity shop at the end of the village. We had great fun in there, trying on almost everything, from old men's suits to old ladies' straw hats. Eventually, though, we did find some clothes that fit us and looked a little older - like the clothes the girls had been wearing - with darker colours. They were a bit tatty in places, but they were alright.

"These will do," I said. "Let's go see my grandad and ask if I can have one of the wooden boxes out of his garden shed."

As we got to my grandad's house, time was pressing on.

"Go in and ask your grandad, then," Thomas said.

"I know, I'm going to," I replied. "I just feel a little awkward that every time I come to see them it's only when I want something."

Just then, I heard my mum shouting, "George, time for tea!"

"I have to go now," I said, and my friends groaned. "We need to hide these clothes. I know, I'll hide them in grandad's coal bunker. If we grab them back later he'll never know they were there."

And so we threw the bag in the bunker.

We agreed that after tea we'd go around and ask my grandad for the box, then we could go and bury it in the woods by the oak tree, leaving only the lid above ground, so we could easily get the clothes in and out.

After tea, we knew we only had a few hours to get the box off my grandad and bury it in the woods. The heat of the day was already fading, and soon our parents would call us in for baths and bedtime.

Thomas came to my house with Patch in tow.

"Why have you got the dog?" I asked.

"Well, because your grandad likes him so much," he explained. "I thought it might distract him as to why you wanted to come down and see him again, so it didn't seem like you were only coming whenever you wanted something."

"Good thinking," I said.

On the way to Grandad's we called on Paul, and then all three of us went together to my grandad's. "Before I knock on the door, Paul, will you grab the bag out of the coal bunker?"

But just as Paul was about to grab the clothes from the bunker, Grandad came to the door.

We all jumped. "Grandad, you gave us a fright!" I laughed.

"Sorry," he replied, not looking very sorry at all. "What are you up to?"

"Nothing, I just thought I'd pop round and see you as I know you liked meeting Thomas's dog earlier."

Grandad laughed and bent down to cuddle and stroke the dog. Patch rolled over onto his back and Grandad rubbed his belly, pulling a treat from his pocket to give him.

"Come on," he said. "You don't fool me, mate. I was young once too, you know. What is it you're after?"

"There's no fooling you, Grandad," I said, laughing too. "We want to bury a treasure chest as part of a game and wondered if you had a wooden box we could have?"

"It just so happens," he said, "I do have a wooden box in my shed that I made not long ago, and you can have it. It's a little large and will take two of you to carry it, but you should get plenty of treasure in there." He smiled and winked at us. "Come in and give me a hand and we'll grab it from the garden shed."

Thomas and Paul waited outside while Grandad, me, and the dog went into the garden to grab the box from the shed. It was about two foot by one foot, with a lid that had two brass hinges and a bolt locking the lid down. It was wood-stained and newly varnished. It was beautiful and well made, and I felt guilty that we were just going to bury it in the ground.

I said, "Are you sure we can have this, Grandad?"

"Yes," he replied. "No problem at all."

"Great!" I said. "Thank you!"

It was perfect for what we needed, I thought to myself.

"Bye then, Grandad!" I called.

"Bye boys," he replied, grabbing Patch's collar for another fuss.

"I think your grandad loves that dog more than I do," Thomas said, as we made our way into the woods.

"I think you're right. I don't know why he doesn't just get one himself if he loves dogs that much," I remarked.

"And it's a bit weird he had a dog treat in his pocket, ready. It's almost as if he was expecting us."

We took turns carrying the box, which was pretty heavy.

As we reached the playing field, Sean and David were walking in the opposite direction, coming from the direction of our rope swing.

"What are you three doing - and what's he doing with that box?" David asked, pointing at Paul, who'd put it down since we'd come to a halt.

"Nothing. It's none of your business," I said.

I was getting fed up with them prowling around the place, asking what we were up to and generally sticking their noses where they didn't belong.

"You want to watch your mouth," Sean threatened, "or we'll tell Dad you've been going down the quarry."

"If you do, I'll tell Dad you've been going down town," I replied.

Sean shoved me in the shoulder and Patch barked and growled at them both.

"Them two are becoming a problem," Paul said as they walked away.

"Yes I know," I said, watching them head off towards home. "It's a pity we couldn't send them across to another dimension!"

We all laughed.

"But seriously, we're going to have to be very careful that they don't follow us one day and see us go through the magic door."

When we got down to the rope swing by the oak tree we started digging a hole, which Patch immediately wanted to help us with. It was very funny that he was so excited - and it made the job a lot easier.

"Thank you, Patch," I laughed, when we were done. "That saved us about half an hour."

We put the box in the hole, then put the bag in it and closed the lid, covering it with branches.

The three of us stood back and examined our handiwork.

"We should call this the vault," I said.

"Yes," Thomas agreed.

"That's a good idea." Paul responded. "Like something out of an adventure story."

"Perfect," I said. "Now, when we go through the magic door we won't look out of place."

Thomas laughed. "No, we'll just look like poor people with our old second-hand clothes with holes in them."

We all giggled at this and I said, "I'd rather look poor than odd."

It was beginning to get dark now, and we all had to go home. On our walk back to the village we planned what we would do. We were so excited - it was like planning to go away on holiday.

We agreed that we'd meet outside my house at 8:30 a.m. and aim to get through the magic door by 9 o'clock. The earlier the better.

"That gives us time to go down and get changed," I said.

"Thomas, it's important that you don't bring the dog this time."

"Yes, I know," he said. "Leave it with me."

I went to bed that night so excited. It was almost like going to bed on Christmas Eve, desperately anticipating the joys of the next day. It was difficult to get to sleep at first, but I knew that I needed a good night's sleep, so I just started imagining my secret life as a secret agent in another dimension, and as my imagination ran on I drifted off to sleep.

CHAPTER SIX

WHERE ARE WE?

The next morning I woke up at 7:30 a.m. sharp.

As usual, Mum asked what I was going to be up to that day.

"Nothing much," I told her. "Just going down to play on the rope swing, hanging out with Paul and Thomas, just making the most of the summer holidays."

"Okay," she said, bringing me my breakfast. "That sounds like fun. Sometimes I wish I was a child again!"

As 8:30 approached, there was a knock at the door. It was Thomas and he had the dog with him.

"Thomas's here," Mum called, giving Patch a pat.

"Okay, Mum - I'm off out now," I shouted as we walked away from the house.

As soon as I'd left, I asked Thomas why he had the dog.

"I know," he complained. "My mum insisted. So, what can we do with him?"

As we walked over towards Paul's house I saw my grandad and grandma walking down the road. I ran over and gave them both a hug.

"Hello, Grandad," I said. "Hello Grandma. You're both out early."

"Yes, it seemed like a beautiful morning, so Grandma and I are going for a walk into town," he replied, stroking Patch's head. "What are you boys up to today?"

"We're off to the woods to play on the rope swing and check up on our treasure chest," I told them.

"Well, why don't we take the dog?" Grandad suggested.

"Yes," Grandma agreed. "That would be nice. Why don't your grandad and I take Patch down into town for a long walk, so you boys don't have to worry about him?"

"Yes!" I shrieked. "I mean yes," I said, in a more normal voice.

"That would be okay, wouldn't it Thomas?" Grandma asked.

Thomas grinned, pleased to have found such an easy solution to our predicament. "Yes of course, if you're sure?"

"Of course we are," Grandad said, holding out his hand. "I wouldn't have offered otherwise. Besides, I think your dog likes me!"

Thomas handed the leash over to Grandad.

"Bye, then," I said as they turned around and walked off. "Have a nice walk!"

"Well, that was lucky," I said, as soon as they were out of earshot.

"Yes," Thomas replied. "Perfect timing."

We met up with Paul and headed down to the old oak tree where we'd buried the chest of clothes the night before.

We were almost skipping with excitement - the adventure was about to begin in earnest!

We decided that we'd leave Paul's watch under the rock and I would wear my watch, like we had the day before. I had to reset it as it was now three hours fast from the last time we passed through the magic door.

Once we were all changed and ready, we stood at the door, looked at each other, and linked arms.

"This is it," Thomas said.

"Yeah," said Paul, looking nervous.

I looked at my watch, and on the stroke of 9 o'clock we all stepped forward through the magic door. As we passed through we heard the girls playing nearby, so we ducked down into the long grass as quickly as we could.

"It's really important they don't see us coming through the magic door," I warned. "We need to be more careful in future."

"Hello, you three!" Iris called. "We can see you hiding in the grass!"

Thomas jumped up like an excited puppy to say hello.

So much for being discreet, I thought. *He must really like her.*

The three of us walked over, joining them by the quarry bank.

"What are you doing today?" Iris asked.

"Nothing," I said. "We're planning to spend the whole day down here. What are you up to?"

Aly said, "We have to run some errands for our mum."

"What errands?" I asked.

"Well," said Iris, "we have to go up the farm to get the milk for the day and then we need to go down town to get some bread from the bakers."

Without thinking, I said, "Why don't you just buy the milk from the shop and then put it in the fridge?"

"Fridge?" Em asked, puzzled. "What's a fridge?"

Thomas quickly pinched my elbow and said to the girls, "Ignore him. He's just being an idiot."

We moved away from the girls and said we were going to throw stones in the quarry, but that if they wanted us to go with them on their errands, we'd be happy to join them.

As we turned to throw stones, just outside the girls' earshot, Thomas said, "We've got to be careful about what we say! You just nearly dropped us in it. We don't know what dimension we're in or whether or not they have the same things we do, so we need to think twice before we speak."

"Yeah, sorry," I mumbled.

"Right," said Paul.

"Well, we're off now," Iris said. "Are you coming?"

"Yes," I said.

Paul said, "Let's go."

As we followed the girls, Thomas made sure we stayed behind them.

I frowned at him and asked, "Why are we following behind them three, Thomas?"

"Think about it," he said. "If they were behind us and we travelled back across into our own dimension, they'd see us disappear."

"But the magic door is over that side of the quarry," I whispered back.

"Yes," he said, "but only as far as we know. For all we know they might be another one, or that one might expand all the way down here."

"I never thought of that," Paul hissed.

"I'm worried," I whispered.

"Just let's be cool, hang back behind them and see what happens," Thomas advised.

Now we were in line with our magic door, but on the other side of the quarry. We all took a breath, grabbed each other by the wrists, and walked forward.

"So far so good," I said, when nothing happened.

Aly turned around and asked, "What's he whispering about?"

"Nothing," Thomas said. "Just chatting."

"Come along, or we'll be here all day."

Thomas, Paul and I shared a look of excitement. This was it, we were leaving the quarry, exploring another world! We couldn't begin to imagine what we might find.

Following the girls, we walked up the hill, out of the quarry and into the woods.

"These woods look familiar, only the trees are a little different," I said. "Some of them are smaller, but there are bigger ones in different places."

"Yes," Thomas replied. "The stream looks a little bigger, but it's the same shape and running along the same path."

"Let's just carry on and follow them to see what happens," I whispered.

Coming out of the woods, we crossed an old, unused field with horses grazing on it.

Paul frowned. "This looks like our football field - but there are bits missing," he whispered.

The girls turned around again, telling us to hurry up as we were walking more and more slowly as things had begun to look weirdly familiar. We walked into the village and shared puzzled looks.

"This looks like our village," said Thomas, "only the houses look newer."

Paul agreed. "I don't think we're in another dimension."

I said excitedly, "I know, I think we've gone back in time!"

But if we were right and we *had* gone back in time, it was no longer a question of *where* we were, but *when*.

"The magic door isn't a link to another dimension, it's a time corridor!" Thomas said.

"This changes things," I told them both. "We need to be extra careful. We need to be sure that we don't change anything."

"Change anything?" Thomas asked. "What do you mean?"

"Think about it," I said. "We've all seen it on TV. If we touch the wrong thing or say the wrong thing it could alter something now and affect something in the future."

The girls were getting further away - and obviously becoming a little frustrated at how slowly we were walking.

"Are you coming, then, or not?" Aly asked.

"No," I said, making up my mind.

Thomas and Paul both turned to me, surprised.

"Why? What are we doing?" Paul asked.

"We need to go back," I said, "we need to come up with a new plan; this is too dangerous.

"I just remembered that Paul needs to go to hospital to see his grandma, so we need to go home!"

"Er, yeah, sorry!" Paul said, cottoning on. "She's really sick."

"Okay," Iris said, sounding somewhat disappointed.

"Will we see you tomorrow?" Aly asked.

"Yes, would you like to meet at the woods?" I asked.

Paul nudged me in the ribs and hissed, "Why not at the quarry?"

"Because there's less likelihood of them seeing us passing backwards and forwards through the magic door if they meet us in the woods."

"Good thinking," Thomas mumbled.

"Okay," Iris agreed. "We'll meet you down by the oak tree near the stream in the woods."

"Which one?" I asked.

"There's a big one down by the stream," said Em. "It has a rope tied to it. We use it as a swing."

"We can't meet in the morning tomorrow," Aly told us. "It's a school day. We'll have to meet you at 4 o'clock."

I realised that their school holidays hadn't started yet.

"Okay, then we'll meet you at 4 o'clock, after school," I shouted as we walked away.

I wondered what date it was if they were still at school. *Another question that needs answering,* I thought to myself as they walked off in the direction of the farm.

"Isn't that strange they've made a rope swing on an oak tree in the woods, just like we did?" I remarked.

We went straight to the tree where we'd built our rope swing and, sure enough, there was a smaller tree with a rope swing on it.

"It's even the same tree!" Paul said, astonished.

"It looks like ours," I said, examining the rope. "It looks a little bit tired and old though, do we trust it?"

Thomas said, "There's only one way to find out!" before taking a run-up. He leapt on the rope swing, swinging it right over the middle of the stream.

"The rope seems just as long as ours, but it doesn't go as far over the stream," Paul observed.

I nodded. "That's because the tree's smaller, because we've gone back in time and the tree is younger than the one we use."

Paul said, "If we've gone back in time, how far back are we?"

"I don't know, but I have an idea," I replied. "Has either of you got a penknife on you?"

"No," said Paul.

Thomas asked, "Why?"

"We can carve our names in the tree and see if they're there in our time," I explained.

"That's something we can bring when we come back. That will be fun," Thomas said. "But what should we do now?"

Paul suggested that we go home. "What do you think, George?"

"Yes," I said. "But tomorrow we need to find out more. Aly said they were at school tomorrow."

"Yes," Thomas said, looking at me strangely, as if he was wondering what I was planning.

On the way back towards the magic door I told them that we needed to find out the exact date and how far we had travelled back.

"We should come back earlier when the girls are at school so we can do some investigating without them," I suggested.

Off we went, back to the magic door, making sure nobody could see us now that we were fully aware that we'd disappear in front of people's very eyes.

When we were back in our own time, Thomas said, "I can get a penknife. My dad has one in his top drawer, by his bed. I'll grab it tonight for tomorrow."

"Okay," I said.

Before we walked home, we went to get changed out of our old clothes. We quickly looked around to make sure we weren't being watched before we changed, and then we put our old clothes back in the box, along with Grandad's watch.

After walking home we sat on the wall at the end of Thomas's garden.

I told them that we needed to come up with a safe plan so we didn't get caught or disrupt anything in the past.

"I've got it!" I said, at last. "We'll get a pen and piece of paper and write a list of rules. We'll call them 'Time Laws' and they must never be broken."

"Yes," Paul agreed, as Thomas ran off into the house to grab a pen and piece of paper.

"This will do," he said, coming back out. "Let's write a title on the front of the notepad: 'Time Travel Laws'."

We sat and passed ideas backwards and forwards, discussing which laws we would use and why. After a little while we all agreed on a set of laws and started writing them down, thinking we were safe as houses with these new laws in place!

Chapter Seven

Time Travel Laws

Finally, we had a list of six laws we must never break:

1. Always stick together when travelling through time.
2. Never tell anyone what we are doing.
3. Never be seen travelling through the time door.
4. Never, ever interfere with the past.
5. Never leave anything in the past.
6. Never bring anything, or anyone, back from the past.

Once they were written down, we swore to one another that these rules must never be broken, or the consequences could be catastrophic.

"Where should we keep this notepad?" Thomas asked, dusting off his hands.

"It's not like we can let anyone see it," said Paul, "or they'll know we're time travellers."

"Don't be silly," I told him. "Think about it. No one would think it's real! They'd think we're just playing a game."

"I suppose you're right," he said, after a moment's thought.

"I'm doing it myself and *I* can't even believe it!" Thomas said.

Just then, Paul's mum shouted him in.

"You need to come in now, Paul! We need to go to the hospital and see your grandma."

"I have to go, now," Paul said to us. "I'll see you tomorrow morning at 8:30?"

We all agreed to meet at 8:30 a.m. and start exploring at 9 o'clock.

When Paul went in, Thomas said, "We'd better go and get Patch back from your grandad."

"Oh yeah! I forgot my grandad had the dog."

As we started walking towards Grandad's house we saw them walking up through the village, which surprised me.

"They're only just getting back now!" I said.

Thomas reminded me that it's still a bit early. He said, "If you think about it, we were playing for hours on the other side, but here only an hour has passed!"

"Ah, yes," I said, remembering the experiment with the watches. "This is going take a little bit of getting used to."

"I know," he replied. "That's why it's important that we always leave a watch under the rock, so we can always check the time to make sure nothing changes with it."

I agreed.

"Hello, boys," Grandma said. "Have you had a good day?"

"Yes," I said. "We've been playing down the woods on the rope swing."

"What tree?" she asked.

"The big oak tree where the branch goes over the stream."

"Yes, I know which one you mean," she said, smiling. "We used to play down there on that one when we were kids."

"What about you, Grandad?" I asked, curious.

"Oh yeah," he replied casually. "Generations of children have played in the woods in the summer and made rope swings over the stream! It's just what kids do."

He passed the leash back to Thomas, who thanked him for walking Patch.

"That's okay, any time," Grandad replied. "I enjoyed taking him for a walk. He's a good dog."

As the day was drawing on, Thomas and I went home.

I was still so excited about what we'd done, but more so about what we were going to do tomorrow. When I walked through the door I had a huge grin on my face.

"Evening George, have you had a good day playing out?" Dad asked.

"Yes, thanks, but I'm absolutely shattered now!" I replied.

He told me to go upstairs and get washed up, ready for tea.

The next morning I woke at around about 7 o'clock. The sun was blazing through the crack in my curtains, so with a quick stretch I jumped up and pulled them open. The sun shone so brightly it nearly blinded me, and when I turned away it left an after-image on my retinas. Behind me in the hallway I heard my mum going downstairs.

By the time I'd joined her, Mum had already made my breakfast. "Make sure you eat it all up before you leave," she told me.

I was so excited to be off I practically inhaled my food, calling farewell over my shoulder.

"Bye!" she said. "Have fun."

Almost skipping down the road with excitement, I walked towards Thomas and Paul's houses, then ran into Paul, who was already walking down the road towards me.

"Morning," he said. "Have you seen Thomas yet?"

"No."

Just then we saw him coming out the house.

"Quickly," he said. "We have to go before my mum makes me take the dog."

Together, we ran to the end of the road, just in case.

"Did you get the penknife?" Paul asked.

"Yes," he replied, pulling a little red-handled Swiss Army knife from his pocket.

"That's a nice-looking knife," I said approvingly.

I just hoped his dad wouldn't notice it had gone missing, or he'd surely be grounded.

We made our way straight down to the rope swing. Then, with a quick look around to make sure nobody was about, we cleared the branches from over the top of the box, grabbed the clothes, and got changed.

"Watch, check," I said.

"Knife, check," Thomas said.

"Time travellers, ready!" Paul said, and we all laughed.

Dressed in our old clothes, we went to the quarry just by the foot of the magic door.

We all had a quick look around and I reminded them of the third law: "We must never be seen. Everyone ready?"

"Yes," Paul replied.

"Let's do it," said Thomas.

So, we stepped forward and through the magic door, making sure that when we emerged on the other side we weren't seen.

"Get down," I whispered.

All three of us ducked down into the long grass.

"What?" Thomas hissed urgently.

"There's an old man over there with his dog, talking to that other man."

Fortunately, the old man had his back to us, but the young man was looking in our direction.

"Do you think he's seen us?" Paul whispered.

"I don't know! Just stay quiet."

We lay in the long grass as we watched the man and his dog walk by in one direction and the young man walk off in the other, towards the rope swing.

"That was too close," I told them. "We need to be extra careful about travelling through the magic door. If he'd seen us, that would have been it!"

"But how are we going to do that?" Thomas asked. "There's no way of telling who'll be on this side until we're through."

"I know!" Paul said. "Why don't we lie on our bellies and crawl through the door when we go through it? That way we'll be crawling from the long grass in one world to the long grass in another. If anybody's in the quarry in either time they won't see us."

"That's a good idea, Paul," I said. "We'll try that when we go back, later on today."

After the men had walked off and were out of sight we all stood up and dusted ourselves off before walking towards the woods and the rope swing, as planned.

"We also have to be careful that people don't think we're playing truant from school, because in the old days they used to send the school board man out looking for kids out of school," I said. "I read it in one of Dad's history books last night."

Luckily, the woods were empty, since everyone was busy with their day-to-day lives.

"Where should we carve our names?" I asked.

"We need to do it where people won't notice it," Thomas said. "We need to do it high up on the oak tree."

"How high?" Paul asked, looking anxious.

I suggested that Thomas got on my shoulders to carve our names.

We knew it would take some time, carving with a little penknife, so we agreed we would just do our initials: 'T', 'G' and 'P'.

I stood with my arms resting against the tree, my feet firmly planted a foot apart, then Paul helped Thomas with a leg up onto my shoulders.

"Pass me the knife, Paul," Thomas asked.

Paul was just about to throw the knife up at Thomas with the blade out, when I shouted, "No!" Paul drew back his arm. "Put the blade away and pass the knife, or you'll have someone's eye out."

Probably mine, I thought.

Paul laughed and said, "Oh yeah, good thinking," as he closed the knife again and passed it up to Thomas.

When Thomas was halfway through the 'P', Paul shouted, "That old man's coming back. Quick, jump down!"

Thomas jumped off my shoulders and quickly dropped the knife into the long grass around the base of the tree. The old man was quickly upon us.

"What are you boys up to, up that tree?" he demanded.

"We're going to climb it," Thomas replied.

"Well you shouldn't be climbing trees, you should be at school!" he told us.

"School is off today," I said to the old man.

"No, it isn't," he replied, looking cross. "My daughters are at school today, so I know you're playing truant. I shall tell the school board about this." He mumbled to himself as he walked away, muttering under his breath, "Children today have no manners!"

"Interfering old busybody," I said, when he'd gone. "What does it have to do with him whether or not we're at school?"

"It's none of his business," Thomas agreed as he climbed back up to finish the 'P'. A few seconds later he shouted out, "Finished!"

"Good!" I said, with some relief as I lowered him down to the ground. "My shoulders are killing me."

All three of us stood back to admire the two-inch-wide letters he'd carved.

"You couldn't have made them any smaller, then?" I joked.

"How long have we been here, George?" Thomas asked, still grinning.

I looked at my watch. "About an hour," I said.

"Let's go back through the magic door and come and have a look at the tree to see if our initials are still on it," Paul suggested.

We all made our way back towards the magic door, but this time we all looked around before leaving the relative shelter of the trees, then we lay down in the grass in line with each other.

We were struggling to link arms while laying down, however, so after a couple of minutes of arguing, we agreed that we'd just make sure that each other's shoulders were touching as we crawled through. It took a little longer, since we had to try quite hard not to lose one another. At last, we made it to the other side, all three of us still together.

"So, we know we don't have to be physically touching each other to get through," Thomas observed. "Just close by."

"I suppose so," I replied.

"That will make things easier," Paul reflected.

With a quick look around to make sure no one was watching, we all stood up.

"Have a look at the time on the watch under the rock," I suggested. "What time is it?" I asked Paul, who had stooped to look.

"It's 9:20," he replied, returning the watch to its hiding place.

"Good," I said. "Let's go down and have a look at the tree."

We were so excited to see the results of our experiment that we ran the whole way there.

"There," Thomas said, pointing upwards.

We all looked up and saw the initials 'T', 'G' and 'P' exactly as Thomas had carved it, but now they were about 9 or 10 feet up the tree - much higher than we had put them.

"How have they got all the way up there?" Paul asked, surprised.

"It's obvious," I said. "The tree has aged and grown taller."

"So, how far back in time would we have to have gone for an oak tree to grow over three foot taller?" he asked.

"I don't know," said Thomas. "A lot of years, probably."

"Well, we can't ask anybody over there the time or date, or they'd think we're mad," I said. "We need to try and find a newspaper or something with today's date on it, up the village," I said.

"And make sure that we don't get caught by anybody, especially the police or school board," Thomas said. "That isn't going to be easy."

"Do you think that school at the bottom of the village is where the girls go?" Paul said suddenly.

There was an old school at the bottom of the village that had been closed for years. The council had taken it on and refitted it, using it as council offices.

"I bet it is," I said. "I bet that's the school. Let's go back through the magic door and sneak up to it, and see what we can find out."

So, off we went, back through the door. Passing through time seemed to become easier and less nerve-wracking the more we did it.

As we huddled in the grass on the other side we listened carefully for a few minutes, looking around to make sure the old man wasn't there.

"The coast is clear," I decided eventually, so the three of us made our way up to the old school at the very end of the village.

This felt far riskier than the things we'd attempted so far, as there were more people around the closer we got to the village.

"Shush," I said to Paul and Thomas, as we hid in the bushes along the road. "Can you hear children playing and shouting?"

"Yes," they both replied.

We stuck our head around the corner and saw that the old neglected school we'd walked past all our lives was bustling with school kids.

This was so exciting; from our perspective, only a few minutes ago the school was run-down and full of council offices, and now here we were, back in a time when the school was so busy.

The school was in a dip, so as we approached it we were able to see over the school wall into the playground, which was separated into two by a large wall. Boys played on one side and girls on the other.

"Look at that!" I said. "The boys and the girls are separated by a wall."

"That's boring," Thomas said. "How would you get a girlfriend?"

Paul and I both laughed.

"You and your girlfriends," Paul scoffed. "You must think you're good-looking."

"Well, I am!" he laughed.

"What are we going to do now?" I asked.

"We need to find an old newspaper or some way of knowing what the date is," Paul reminded us.

"Wait a minute," Thomas said, as we were turning away. "I can see Iris."

"Where?" I asked.

"Over there, in the corner of the playground."

I spotted her among a group of other girls. We began to wave, trying to get her attention and beckoning her over to the gate while at the same time trying not to be seen by the teachers.

Eventually I gave up, deciding it was worth the risk. "Iris!" I shouted. "Over here."

Iris looked up, a huge grin on her face, and made her way over to the gate.

"What're you doing here?" she asked. "Why aren't you at school? If the teachers see you, you'll be in big trouble."

"We go to another school and our school is off today," I lied.

She didn't look like she believed me, but she didn't say anything about it.

"What are you doing here?" she asked again.

"We're just playing out," Thomas said, "and I wanted to come and see you."

Iris smiled at him. "That's nice. I'm glad you did."

As they were talking, I came up with a cunning plan to find out what the date was - and I must admit, it was a very clever idea.

"Iris," I said. "Could you settle an argument between Paul and me?"

She said, "I'll try."

"What year did World War One finish?" I asked.

"The war?" she said, puzzled. "There's only been one World War and it ended in 1918. Why?"

Without answering her, Paul asked, "So how many years has it been since the war ended?"

"Well, work it out!" she said, laughing. "If it ended in 1918 and it's now 1936, it ended 18 years ago."

She suggested that maybe we should go to school as we couldn't work out simple maths and then laughed at us again. Just then, a teacher walked out of the nearest door and began ringing a hand-held bell.

"I have to go," she said. "Will I see you after school?"

"Yes," Thomas replied. "We'll meet you down by the rope swing, as planned."

"1936!" I gasped, as we walked away from the school, being careful not to be spotted by the teacher. "We're in 1936! That's 50 years back in time!"

This was so exciting. Although we'd known we were back in time, knowing just when made us a little more confident.

"Let's go back to the rope swing," I suggested.

We all agreed. It was tricky, trying to stay out of sight of people. We didn't want to get caught. As we made our way through the hedgerows on the edge of the village, we saw a policeman with his back to us. He was talking to the same man we'd seen in the quarry and the woods that morning.

"Hurry, you two, the police are there!" I said. "We need to get out of sight before he turns around and sees us."

We ran off into the woods, not stopping until we were sure we were unobserved. "That was close," I said.

Feeling safe again, we walked back to the tree, discussing the year.

"George!" Thomas said suddenly. "Don't most of your family come from this area?"

"Yes, they do," I replied. "We've lived around here forever."

"So, there's a chance that you might know some of the people we'll bump into?"

I was stunned. "You're right! We're going to have to be extra careful and be sure we don't break law number 4 - don't change the past."

The boys nodded.

"What should we do?" I asked, a big smile on my face. "Should we wait here in 1936, or go back to 1986?"

"It sounds strange when you say it like that," Thomas said.

"I suppose," I said. Something had occurred to me. "People might hear us talking so we need to come up with names for the different times."

"I know what you mean," Paul said. "How about we call 1986 'home' for example, and here in 1936 could be called 'away'. Is this what you mean, George?"

"Yes," I said.

"Then that's what we'll do," said Thomas.

My stomach rumbled. "I'm hungry," I said.

"Me too," Thomas agreed. "Let's go home and get some lunch, then come back down to meet the girls after they get out of school?"

"Good idea," Paul replied.

Chapter Eight

Who's That?

As we started to approach the magic door, I caught a movement out of the corner of my eye. I whispered to them both, "Get down."

"What?"

"Why?"

As we all slammed ourselves down into the long grass, I peeked my head over the top of it. Just then, the boy looked over, so I ducked my head back down as quickly as I could.

"There's a boy over there by the quarry wall!" I hissed.

Cautiously, Thomas and Paul both looked over the top of the long grass, over by the quarry wall.

"Where?" Thomas asked. "I can't see anyone!"

I popped my head back up and he was gone.

"He was over there," I said. "He looked straight at me."

"There's no one there now. He must have gone," Thomas said.

"What did he look like?" Paul asked.

"He just looked like a boy about our age," I told them. "He was playing over by the quarry wall."

Ordinarily, they would have just said I was seeing things, but under the circumstances we had to be extremely careful that we weren't being watched and that nobody knew what we were up to.

Slowly, we made our way towards the magic door, keeping a close eye out to make sure no one was watching us.

As we approached the door Paul asked, "Where did you see him?"

"Just there, down by the wall," I said, pointing.

We all had a good look around. I didn't see anyone. I shrugged at the others and shouted, "Hello! Is anyone there?"

But nobody replied. There was clearly no one there, so we lay down in the grass and crawled through the magic door. Once we were through, we went to change into our normal clothes.

As we walked up towards the village I was wondering who it was I saw playing. He seemed oddly familiar, but I didn't know who he was and I thought I knew everyone our age who lived nearby. Perhaps someone had a cousin visiting for the week, or something.

I had all these questions running through my head: Who was that boy? Did he see me looking at him? Why didn't I recognise him?

I'm sure he saw me, I thought to myself.

"What's wrong with you?" Thomas asked, after a while. "You're being very quiet for a change."

"Nothing," I replied. "I'm just thinking about that boy. I'm sure I recognised him, I just can't think where from!"

"Who do you think he was?" Paul asked.

"I don't know... I just don't know!"

I told them I didn't know, but deep down I had a suspicion that really I *should* know, and I knew he'd seen *me* because he'd had a very confused look on his face when I spotted him.

"That's somebody else we need to look out for then," Paul said.

By this time, we'd arrived in the village. We went our separate ways and agreed to meet back up in an hour.

As soon as I walked through the door, my mum was waiting with my lunch.

"Hello George," Mum said. "What's wrong with you?"

"Nothing," I replied, surprised. "What makes you think something's wrong?"

"Just something about your face. You look puzzled or confused, it's not the happy face that left this morning," she told me. "Have you had a falling out with your friends?"

"No," I said. "We've had a really good morning. I'm hungry."

While I was eating my lunch, my dad came in from the garden. "Hello George!"

"Hi Dad, what're you up to?"

"Just doing some gardening, keeping out your mother's way." He grinned.

"I heard that, you cheeky beggar!" Mum shouted through.

"Only joking, love," he said, laughing.

I asked him to tell me about the school at the bottom of the village and how long it had been closed.

"Oh," he said, surprised. "It was shut maybe 12 years ago. Just before you were born, in fact. Why?"

"No reason," I lied. "Just curious, that's all. Did you go there as a little boy?"

"Yes," he said. "And my mum and dad before me, and maybe even my grandad, but I'm not sure about that. Why? What's this fascination about the past, all of a sudden?"

"Nothing," I said quickly, thinking he must be on to me. "I was only wondering about it. That's all."

I thought I'd better go before I put my foot in it.

After lunch I went around to call on Thomas and Paul. Thomas came out as I approached his house; he must have been watching for me through the window.

As we walked towards Paul's house, we saw him coming out with his parents and walking towards their car.

"Are you coming out, Paul?" I asked.

"No," his mum said, answering for him. "We're going to the hospital to see his grandma. She's very poorly."

"Sorry to hear that," I said, though Paul had told us earlier.

Paul walked over to us and whispered, "It's okay, you can bend law one and you both can go together without me. You don't want to upset the girls by not turning up."

"You sure?" Thomas asked.

"Yes, just tell me all about it when I get back."

We agreed, telling him we'd see him later, then Thomas and I went off to the quarry together, stopping at the woods to get changed.

As we approached the magic door we had a good look around, then we lay down in the grass and crawled through the door on our bellies for as far as we could out into the long grass, making sure nobody could see us.

"Coast clear," I said as we stood up and made our way down towards the oak tree.

I was looking back to see if I could see the boy again.

"What are you looking for?" Thomas asked.

"That boy I saw earlier."

"Do you think you might be able to see him through another magic door?" Thomas asked. It had obviously been on his mind, too.

"I'm starting to wonder!"

He grinned. "Could this day get any more exciting?"

"I don't know," I said, grinning back. "But it means we have to make sure - if there *is* another magic door - that we don't accidentally go through it and end up in a different time."

We carried on down towards the rope swing, where we saw the girls already waiting for us.

"Hi boys," Aly said. "Where's Paul?"

"His grandma isn't well," I said. "She's had to go into hospital, so he's gone to visit her."

"Send him our love," Em said.

"We're going down into town," Iris said. "We need to go to the shops for my mum. Do you want to come with us?"

"Yes!" Thomas replied, very quickly and excitedly.

"Okay then," Iris said, amused. "But you're not going to go back home halfway there again? Like you did before."

"No," I told her, "we have all the time in the world!"

I winked at Thomas, who had to stifle a laugh.

Off we went through the woods and up across the old field.

"Here we are, Thomas," I whispered, unable to contain my excitement. "We're going to our village in the past."

It was so awesome! We were going to see our village, 50 years in the past, and see how people used to live. This was way better than throwing rocks at bottles in the quarry!

Through our excitement, it dawned on us that they were leading us towards their house.

"Are we going straight to the town?" I asked Iris.

"No," she said. "We have to go home first to get some money from my mum."

We walked behind the girls, who were laughing amongst themselves, while we looked around in total amazement at the buildings. Some were missing, and some we didn't recognise. The rest looked so new compared to what we remembered from home.

"You two stay here," Em said. "If our mum sees you, she won't let us go down town."

"Why not?" I asked.

"Because you're boys, so wait here."

We watched Iris, Em and Aly all go into number 7.

I remarked to Thomas, "I wonder who lives in number 7 back home."

"I don't know," he said. "My family aren't from around this village. Nor is Paul's. Only yours."

My mouth fell open in surprise. "That means I really might get to actually meet my family!" For some reason this was only just hitting me, despite our earlier conversation.

"Yes," he agreed. "But you have to be careful if you do bump into any of your family! It's important that you don't let them know or find out what we're up to. Also, you shouldn't interact with them too much, or you might change the future - you said that yourself."

"I know," I said, "I'll be careful."

Just then, we heard a dog barking and whining nearby.

"That sounds like Patch!" Thomas said.

"It does a bit," I said. "But Patch's 50 years in the future, so it can't be him."

The dog continued to bark and when I looked across the village I saw two boys with a dog. I pointed them out to Thomas as the two boys ran off, pulling the dog behind them.

"It even looks like Patch!" Thomas said, with a laugh.

"Well, I'm sure they made more than one Jack Russell!" I said, laughing too.

CHAPTER NINE

MY FAMILY

A few minutes later, Iris and Aly came out. We expected them to wait for Em, but they didn't.

"Where's Em?" I asked, when they drew level with us.

Aly told us that Em had had to stay in and help their mum with some housework.

"Mum?" I asked. "I thought that was Iris's mum's house?"

"Yes," Aly said, giving me a funny look. "It's all of our mum's house. We're sisters."

I couldn't believe what I was hearing. "Sisters!" I repeated.

"Yes, didn't you know?" Iris asked.

"No," I replied, feeling foolish. "I thought you were all just friends."

"What difference does it make?" asked Aly.

"None," I said nervously, "I was just surprised."

"What's up with you?" Thomas asked. "You're acting all strange. So they're sisters, what of it?"

I told the girls Thomas and I would catch them up and we'd follow behind because I just wanted to ask Thomas something.

"Okay," Aly said and looked at Iris with a grin. "I bet they're talking about us. Thomas fancies you."

"Shut up, Aly!" Iris said as Aly walked off, laughing.

When they were safely out of earshot Thomas asked, "What's up? What's the matter?"

"They're sisters!"

"Yes, and?" Thomas asked. "What's the big deal?"

"I think that Iris might be my grandma and Aly is my Auntie Alice and Em is my Auntie Emma!" The words came out in a tumble, and for a moment Thomas just stared at me.

Then his face turned white. "Oh no! What do we do?"

"I don't know! If they are, how we can find out?"

"Ask Aly what her proper name is?" he suggested.

"Yes, I can do that, but what if she says her name is Alice? What would I do? I think I'd pass out."

Thomas told me not to panic and stop being a baby, and I didn't want to look bad in front of my friend, so I shouted, "Aly! We were just wondering what Aly was short for - or is that your full name?"

"No, silly," she replied. "It's Alice, but my friends call me Aly for short."

I stopped dead in my tracks and went cold; I thought I'd been prepared for what I was about to hear but the shock still stunned me.

"What's the matter with you?" she asked. "You look like you've just seen a ghost!"

"It's nothing," I muttered, almost under my breath.

Iris asked Thomas, "What's the matter with your friend? Is he okay? It looks like he's going to pass out."

"No, he's fine," Thomas replied, trying to brush it off. "He's just being silly." When they looked away, he turned to me and hissed, “Pull yourself together! Or they’re going to know something’s up.”

I came around from being stunned and carried on walking, still a few feet behind the girls.

Once I’d recovered a little, I said to Thomas, “I can’t believe this is my grandma and my great aunt Alice. They’re almost the same age as us, walking just feet away.”

This was the most bizarre feeling and situation I had ever experienced. It was like something out of a book!

“What are you both whispering about?” Iris asked, still suspicious.

“Nothing,” I said, as we ran and caught up with them.

Nervous and excited, we walked out of the village, past the old school and down the road towards the town, which was around a mile away.

Thomas and I were looking all around us, the way that people do on holiday when they’ve never been to a place before.

Iris said, “Why are you both always looking around? Are you looking for someone?”

“Or is somebody looking for you?” Aly asked, raising an eyebrow.

“No,” I said, thinking on my feet. “I thought I heard Paul coming.”

“I thought Paul was going to see his grandma?” Iris said.

“Yes, that’s why I wasn’t sure whether or not it was him I heard.”

“Quick thinking,” Thomas murmured, as the girls turned away again. He patted me on the back. “Now let’s try and act normal.”

"Try and act normal?" I repeated. "Easier said than done! I can hardly contain my excitement!"

"I know what you mean," he said. "I'm the same. I think if I get another shock, I'll wet myself!" He laughed.

I wanted to ask Aly and Iris a million questions, but I had to contain myself; I had to gather the information slowly so as not to arouse suspicion. We caught back up to them.

"So, Aly. How old are you?"

"11 and a half," she said.

"And what about you, Iris?"

"I'm 10 and Em is 13."

"Me and Thomas are both 10," I told them.

"Paul too," Thomas added. "But George has older brothers."

"I bet they're real pains," said Aly, pulling a face.

"You have no idea," said George.

We were now approaching the town, and Thomas and I were having a hard time simply not gawping at everything that was different - and everything that was the same.

"What do you have to get for your mum, Iris?" I asked.

"A loaf of bread and some ham," she replied. "Do you need to get anything while you're here?

"No, thank you," I said, knowing that we had no money from the past.

We walked into the bakery shop and it was like something out of a museum we'd been to on a school trip. The smell of fresh bread was amazing. We always got our bread from the shops, already baked, so it was something I'd never smelled before.

The wooden floorboards were dusty and anything that didn't smell of fresh bread had a clean, fresh aroma.

Thomas and I looked around the shop, trying not to look too much like tourists, taking everything in. Everything looked different: the light switches, the lights hanging down from the ceiling, the people walking past and around the town, going about their business. It was the past - half a century distant - and yet happening in front of our very eyes.

Iris asked the man behind the counter for a loaf of bread, so he took one off the stand and wrapped it in paper. It was a very strange sight for me. I thought bread only came in bags. When she handed him the money he jotted the numbers down on a piece of paper before passing her change back.

Change out of a penny, I thought to myself, with a jolt.

I said to Thomas, in an undertone, "If I brought all my savings here I'd be rich."

"I know," he said. "If only."

"We need to go to the butchers next, across the road," Aly said.

As we walked out of the bakers, I noticed the second-hand shop next door. I was just thinking to myself that we should pop in there and see if we could buy some shoes that looked like they were from 1936 when I stepped out into the road.

I heard the urgent 'ding' of a bell, then Aly shouted, "Stop! Get back!"

A man grabbed me roughly by my arm and pulled me directly out of the path of the tram that was about to run me down.

It was the man we'd seen talking to the old man at the quarry and the policeman in the village earlier on. The tram passed right in front of my eyes as the man let go of my arm and walked off before I had the chance to thank him.

"You were just very nearly run down!" Aly said.

"Are you alright?" Iris asked.

Thomas said, "He's okay."

"What's the tram doing down here?" I asked.

Aly looked, rolled her eyes, and said, "What do you mean? The trams have been coming down here for years."

"I know," I said, still shaken. "Only joking."

Thomas looked at me. "There hasn't been a bus or tram car down this road for as long as I can remember. We'll have to be more careful," he whispered.

I told Thomas the man who saved my life was the same man we'd seen earlier.

"I know," he replied. "I recognised him, and just as well he was there, or you'd be squashed flat right now."

We crossed over the road to the butcher's shop. It was strange seeing rabbits and pheasants hanging in the window, and when we went in it had a real smell of fresh raw meat about it. There was sawdust on the floorboards beneath our feet, some of it clumping with the spilled blood.

"What can I get you girls?" the shopkeeper asked, clearly recognising them.

Aly replied, "We just need cooked ham, thanks."

"No problem. How much?" the butcher asked. "The usual amount?"

"Yes, please," she replied.

"How is my sister?" he said, as he worked.

"She's fine," Aly replied.

I turned to Thomas and whispered, "He must be my great uncle."

Thomas grinned. "Is there anybody around here that isn't related to you?" he chuckled.

"I know," I replied. "It's going to be difficult trying not to bump into people."

"And who are these boys?" the butcher asked.

"These are our friends from the village," Iris replied.

He looked at Aly and said, "Oh yes? I don't recognise them."

"Who's your mum and dad?" he asked.

Before we could answer, Iris came to the rescue. "They just moved there," Iris said. "You won't know them."

"Alright," he said. "But be careful about hanging around with unfamiliar boys. And you be nice to these little ladies," he added, pointing at us with his cleaver.

When we left the shop a few minutes later, I asked Iris, "Is your uncle okay with you hanging out with us?"

"Yes, and he won't tell our mum, but it's best we keep our friendship a secret, or we'd be in trouble for hanging out with boys. Especially runaways, like you!"

"Yes!" Aly said, with some excitement. "You must be runaways. We've been talking about it and it's the only explanation."

"We know you're not from the village and your clothes are a little bit scruffy," said Iris.

"We're not runaways," I said hurriedly. "We're really from the next village over, Ash Meadows. It's just our parents don't have a great deal of money and that's why our clothes are scruffy."

I'm not sure if they believed us, but they went along with it.

"Come on," Iris said, with some sarcasm. "Let's walk back to the village before anybody else starts asking questions, or George gets himself run down and killed."

Thomas laughed. "Yeah, you have no idea how much trouble that would cause!"

We started walking back towards the village, making sure we kept a good eye on the time, but we knew we had loads left as we had three hours to every one back home.

The girls said that when we got back to the village they needed to drop the bread and ham back at home so we'd have to meet in the woods by the rope swing.

We walked together, but this time Iris walked with Thomas and Aly and I brought up the rear.

Aly said, "I think Iris likes Thomas."

"I think Thomas likes Iris as well," I admitted. "I've never seen him so giddy around a girl before."

Deep down I was thinking, *Please, Aly. Please, don't ask me out - I've got no idea how I would say no!*

Fortunately she said, "Don't worry about me, though. I don't think you're my type!"

I gave her a smile, thinking I'd had a lucky escape, but as we walked on I wondered what was wrong with me - why wasn't I her type?

As we got to the village the girls headed off.

"Off you go, we'll see you down the rope swing in about half an hour!" Aly called over her shoulder.

Iris and Aly linked arms and walked off together towards the house, while me and Thomas walked back towards the woods.

"What were you and Iris talking about?" I asked.

"Nothing," he replied casually. "We were just chatting. I feel like I really like her. We get on well."

"Just don't forget we can't do anything to change the past."

We arrived at the oak tree rope swing and started playing, waiting for the girls to come back.

Soon, half an hour had passed and we were starting to think they weren't coming, but then we heard them talking and walking towards us. It was still just Aly and Iris.

"No Em?" I asked.

"No," Aly replied. "She's still helping our mum."

"Let's play on the rope swing, then," I said.

"Me first!" Aly replied.

This was bizarre for me, watching my Great Aunt Alice and Grandma playing on a rope swing with me, acting like little boys.

"You three can pull me out and swing me as hard as you can over the stream," she said. "The one to get the furthest out can be the winner."

Thomas and I pulled back on either side of the half-branch she was sitting on and give her a big push over the water.

I laughed as she whooped and giggled. I looked at Thomas and said, "This must be where I get my competitiveness from."

We all took turns swinging out over the water. We had so much fun, I didn't want the day to end, but eventually it did.

"What time is it?" Aly asked me, as I was the only one wearing the watch.

"It's nearly 7 o'clock," I replied.

"We should go, Iris," Aly said. "Or we'll be in trouble and not allowed back out."

"Are you going to be okay?" I asked.

"Yes," she replied. "Only we have to be in by 7 o'clock, so we really need to go." She shouted back to us as they ran off, "See you tomorrow?"

Thomas nearly broke his neck to shout back, "Absolutely!"

"I suppose we'd better get back now, too," I said to Thomas.

We started walking back, working out what time it was as we went.

"It's probably still only early afternoon," I said.

"Good," Thomas replied. "I'm starving. We've been here all day with no food, but our parents think we've only been gone three hours since lunch."

We agreed that we needed to come up with a long-term plan, or at least get some money for the past so we could buy food when we were there.

As we approached the magic door I said to Thomas, "We should look out for that boy you saw, just in case he sees us travelling through."

"How do you want to do this, then?" Thomas said.

"We'll sneak up, crouch down as low as we can until we get into the long grass, and then crawl up towards the magic door and have a good look around."

"Okay," Thomas said. "Let's do that."

As we started crouching I said, "Stop! Look over there, across the water. I see him lying on the bankside."

"Yes," he said. "I see him."

"Who do you think it is?" Thomas asked.

"I'm not sure, but we should try to avoid being caught by him when going through the magic door."

As if he'd heard us, the boy turned and looked at us; we both lay down flat on our bellies.

"I can see you!" we heard him shout.

I sat up, deciding it would be weirder if we pretended we weren't there. "Hello!" I shouted, but he ignored me and turned back around to do whatever it was he was doing.

I think he was playing with a catapult, or something.

"Quickly," I said. "While he's not looking, let's crawl through the door."

We crawled through the magic door as fast as we could. Once we were home, we climbed to our feet.

"Grab the watch, Thomas," I said. "See what time it is."

We rolled the rock over and saw that it was 2 o'clock.

To my dismay, when we walked towards the oak tree we found Sean and David playing on the rope swing.

"Oh no," I said. "There's Sean and David."

"That's not the end of the world," Thomas said. "They didn't see us come through the door."

"I know, but look at what we're wearing," I said. "We're wearing old-fashioned, tatty clothes, and they're going to start asking questions."

Just then Sean looked up and shouted over, "What are you wearing? You look like a pair of scruffs."

They both laughed and David said, "We've been sent down to get you!"

"What are we going to do, Thomas?" I asked. "We can't go home like this! My mum and dad will want to know why we're wearing these clothes, and we can't get changed here in front of Sean and David, or they'll find out where our secret buried box is."

"Just tell your mum that we've been playing in fancy dress and that you got the clothes from my house," said Thomas, thinking quickly. "I'll tell my mum the same and we'll just have to hope they don't talk to each other about it."

We didn't really have any other options.

Thomas went off to his house as I walked home.

Straightaway when I walked in the door my mum and dad both looked at me and frowned.

"What on earth are you wearing?" Mum asked.

"Thomas and I were playing fancy dress," I explained, self-consciously. "We were pretending we were runaways, living down in the woods."

"Well I hope the clothes you left the house in are clean. Where are they?"

"Around Thomas's," I said, hoping wildly that she didn't send me over to get changed. How would I explain that?

Chapter Ten

What Time is It? The New Law

A while later I went to call on Thomas, and when I knocked, his mum came to the door.

"I see you're dressed in fancy dress, too," she said, amused but stern. "You two look a right pair! I've told Thomas he needs to go over to your house and get changed into his clothes."

"Yes," I replied. "That's why I've called on him."

Thomas, eager to be off, squeezed past her.

"Don't forget the dog!" his mum said, passing over Patch's lead.

As soon as we were safely out of sight, we started discussing the clothing situation.

"We might have to change our tactics," I said, "and find somewhere else to keep our clothes - somewhere my brothers can't show up and spoil things."

"But where?" Thomas asked. "It's not like we can guarantee they won't come into the woods."

We were quiet then until we reached the trees, trying to think of somewhere else that things could be stashed.

On the way down to the oak tree I asked Thomas, "What time do you think it would be if we went through the magic door now?"

He replied, "Well, we've been here for one hour, and we left there at about 7 o'clock, so it might be 10 o'clock at night there."

"No, I think you're wrong!" I said. I'd been considering this. "I think the time is only slower when we're there. If we go through the magic door now the time will be 3 o'clock - the same time it is now!"

"If that's true, if we stay there until 6 o'clock their time and then come back, it will still only be 4 o'clock here," Thomas reasoned.

We agreed to try the theory out and see if I was right.

"But if I *am* right," I said, "then we could double or triple the time we can spend down there by just popping back and forth."

"Let's not get too carried away," he replied. "Let's try it first, but when you say it like that it sounds possible!"

"We should still go down and get changed, just in case we get called back in," he said. "And then when we go through the magic door we'll just stay at the quarry, out of people's way. That way it won't matter that we're wearing more modern clothes."

"What are we going to do about the dog?" I asked.

"I don't know," Thomas said. "Do you think we could take him through?"

"Would that not break one of our laws? Not telling anyone?" I joked and we both laughed.

"I'm sure Patch won't tell anyone," Thomas said.

Once we'd changed we grabbed both watches before setting off to the magic door.

"Okay," I said. "It's nearly 3:00 p.m., and if I'm correct it will be 3:00 p.m. on the other side of the magic door too."

"Yes," Thomas said, frowning. "But how would we know it was 3:00 p.m. there and not 10 o'clock at night?"

We both stared around, looking for inspiration, then I clapped my hands together, making Patch jump and bark. "I've got it, we can make a sundial!"

"Sundial?" he asked. "What do you mean?"

I explained, "It's got to do with where the sun is at particular times of day. As you can see, at this time and position the sun is behind me, casting a shadow directly in front of me. So, if we go through the magic door and the shadow is in the same place, then we know it's the same as it is here - if not, then it's a different time of day."

"Very clever!" Thomas said.

"I know! I'm a genius, what can I say?" I laughed.

I did feel rather clever for coming up with the idea.

On the other side of the magic door we could see there was no one around the quarry, so we stood up.

"There it is, Thomas," I said. "Our shadows are in exactly the same place as they were when we were on the other side! This must mean it's 3 o'clock here, too."

"I guess you're right, clever-clogs," he said.

This left us with a new problem. We needed to spend three hours on this side of the door, but we couldn't risk bumping into anyone dressed the way we were, in clothes from the 1980s.

"Let's go for a walk, deep inside the woods," Thomas suggested. "And then if anyone comes we're in the best place to hide."

"Okay then, let's go."

We set off immediately, forgetting at once that we'd agreed to stay at the quarry.

"Come on, Patch," Thomas said, pausing.

"What's up with the dog?" I asked.

"I don't know," he said. "He's shivering - it's like he's scared and doesn't want to move."

Dogs have a sixth sense, I thought, *and we don't.*

"He must know that something's not quite right," I said.

"I still get chills down my spine when I come the other side of the magic door, it's so unreal," Thomas said. "I suppose it's no surprise that Patch should be upset about it."

It took a little time to coax him forward, but after cajoling him for a minute or two he slowly started making his way away from the magic door. It quickly became clear that the further away from the door we got, the more relaxed he became.

"It must just be the magic door that scared him," Thomas said. "He's calmed right down."

We strolled into the woods, making the most of the good weather and our extra time, but it wasn't long before Patch started to bark and pull on his lead, trying to drag us towards the stream.

"Be quiet, Patch!" Thomas said.

"What's he barking at?" I asked.

"I don't know, but he wants to be down by the stream."

We crouched down, and over by the stream we saw the old man walking his dog - the same old man who told us off for not being at school.

"This is all we need," I muttered. "That miserable, grumpy old man seeing us again."

Just then, his dog started barking and pulling towards us. Patch responded in kind.

"We need to go, run!" I shouted.

We ran in the opposite direction, pulling Patch behind us.

"I can see you!" the old man shouted after us. "I've told the school board that you were playing truant and they're going to come looking for you!"

"Mind your own business, you grumpy old man!" I shouted back as we ran off.

"What are you doing?" Thomas asked, panting.

"Well," I said, "what business is it of his? Grumpy old busybody."

"Yes, but we're not supposed to draw attention to ourselves or upset anybody," he reminded me. "We can't risk changing the future."

"What, by telling an old man that he's grumpy? Anyway, he probably gets called that all the time."

But yes, I conceded, when we slowed down enough to think, he was right.

"We just need to stay out of his way, and out of the way of the school board," I grumbled. Then I frowned. "I've just thought of something," I said to Thomas.

"What?" he asked.

"Hear me out and see if it makes sense to you," I said.

I took a deep breath. "When we left the girls here it was 7 o'clock, and when we went back it was 2 o'clock, yes?"

"Yes," he said.

"Right, so we've come back here at 3 o'clock in the afternoon."

"Yeah," he said, not following me.

"Well, think about it - the girls will be in their house while we're waiting outside."

"This is hurting my head," Thomas said, and I nodded. "I know what you're trying to say, but I can't get my head around it."

"I know," I said. "But is this 3:00 p.m. today or is it 3:00 p.m. tomorrow - I mean, the day after we last saw them?"

I could see Thomas was trying to work it out by the puzzled look on his face.

"I think it's probably today, still," he said. "Because if it was tomorrow, more time would have to have passed back home before we came back through."

"How about we test it?" I suggested. "If we sneak into the village we'll be able to see ourselves waiting for the girls to finish talking to their mum."

"If you're right about this," Thomas said, "then we need to make it a law - that we only cross the magic door once a day for only a few hours of our time. 10 hours of this time at most."

"Why?" I asked him.

"Well, think about it," he said. "Think about the TV programmes you've seen. If we do bump into ourselves, it could be catastrophic to the space-time continuum."

"You really have been watching too much TV," I laughed.

"Yes, I know. But what if the TV's correct?" he pointed out, looking troubled. "What happens if we bump into each other in the past? Is it worth the risk?"

"Okay," I agreed, "but I still think we need to go up to the village and see if we can see ourselves walking off with the girls. That way we'll know for sure."

So, we played around in the woods a little longer, and as 4 o'clock approached, we made our way towards the village.

"We'll hide here in this yard. It doesn't look like anybody's living here," I said, looking around.

"Good idea," he replied.

We sat in the yard of an old, empty house (that I didn't recognise from the future) for around about five minutes, until Patch started pulling on his lead and whining.

"What's wrong with the dog?" I asked.

"I don't know," Thomas said, as Patch started barking and going crazy.

We both popped our heads above the wall in time to see our earlier selves standing outside Aly and Iris's house. Then, just as they looked around, we quickly ducked our heads behind the wall.

I said to Thomas, "I think that's us!"

"I think you're right and the dog's going mad because he can see us."

We popped our heads up one last time and saw the two boys looking over.

"Run!" I said.

Thomas and I ran off, pulling the dog behind us. All the while he was still barking and trying to get over to our other selves over the road.

"That was too close," I said. "Remember earlier on when we were waiting for the girls and we saw two boys and heard the dog? Well, that was us!"

"Yes!" he replied. "I remember. We need to get back to the magic door and make sure this never happens again."

We ran the whole way, and when we got to the quarry we made our way towards the magic door, crouching down and looking around to make sure we weren't seen.

The dog started whining the closer we got, so we quickly passed through.

"We're home," I said, relieved.

"Good," Thomas replied. "What time is it?"

"It's only just gone 4 o'clock."

"Come on, then," I said. "Let's go and hide the watches in the box, then go and call on Paul and see how his grandma is. Then we can tell him about what just happened."

We got to the village and called on Paul, but when he come to the door he was really sad.

"What's up, mate?" I asked.

"My grandma, she died," he said, bursting into tears.

Thomas and I shared a horrified look. "We're really sorry to hear that mate," I said.

"Thank you," he replied.

His mum came to the door, to see who was there.

"Go out and play with your friends," she told him. "It might help take your mind off things."

"Okay, Mum," he replied sadly.

Together, we walked slowly to the end of the road, Patch bouncing along at our feet. Suddenly all the fun we'd been having seemed like a distant memory.

"Do you want to talk about your grandma?" Thomas asked. "Or if not, we could talk about what we did today?"

"Go on, then," he said. "Tell me about your day. It might take my mind off Grandma."

"So, when we went to meet the girls, everything went okay at first," I told him, as we walked. "But get this! They're only my grandma, my auntie Alice, and auntie Emma!"

Paul stopped and stared at me, clearly shocked and intrigued. At least it seemed to have cheered him up a little.

"So, you've met your grandma and your aunts in the past? That must've been really strange!"

"You're telling me," I said. "But it gets even more strange."

We told him about the experiment we performed on timing, about how we'd seen our earlier selves, and about the boy at the quarry.

Paul agreed we should avoid running into ourselves in the past.

He sighed. "I wish I'd spent more time with my grandma," he said sadly. "I miss her already. I wish I knew more about her. I've known her for 10 years and I've never asked any questions about her life, or what she used to get up to as a small child. Even who my real grandad was. I wish I could go back!"

Suddenly, he looked directly at the both of us.

I knew exactly what he was going to say.

"Could we go back in time and meet my grandma?" he pleaded. "I want to get to know her better and with this new gift, there's no reason I can't. Come on, why not?"

"You know this is too dangerous," I said, sad that we couldn't help him. "It's one of the laws that we don't change anything in the past."

"What about you?" he demanded. "It's okay for you to go back and talk to your family, but not for me?"

He was quite right! Why should we be any different?

"Where did your grandma grow up?" Thomas asked.

"I don't know," he said, but he was already smiling. He knew we were going to help him now. "I'll find out! It's not far from here, I'm sure, because she had the same accent as us."

"You find out from your mum and we'll make up a plan where we can go and meet her," I said.

"You'll also need to find out how old she is, because the time door only takes us back to 1936," Thomas pointed out.

Greatly cheered, he told us to leave it with him and he would find out everything there was to know about her.

"When do you go on holiday?" I asked.

"Next week," he said. "So we need to go and find her before then. We don't know how long the magic door will stay there."

"No," I said. "That might be too soon for us to properly prepare. We need to plan this better. Go on your holiday and know that you have something to look forward to when you get back. You can use the time to find out all you can about her from your mum. After all, we do have the gift of time!"

We laughed.

"Once you have her full name and childhood address we'll find her and let you know how we get on."

"Okay," he said reluctantly. "That's probably best, you're probably right… but can you try and find out who my grandad was while you're there?"

"That will be difficult," I pointed out, "as your grandma will only be around our age in 1936. She might not even have met him yet."

"Okay," he replied. "I suppose you're right, just find out as much as you can."

Paul's mum called him back in, but we stopped him because he had a huge smile on his face.

"Paul," Thomas said, "you can't go in all happy and excited! Your mum and dad will think you're either being selfish or that you don't care that your grandma's died."

"You're right… I need to think of something sad," he said, wiping the smile from his face. "Thanks again."

We watched him go, both of us perturbed about what Paul had in mind.

Thomas looked at me. "I know what you're trying to do, and it's a lovely gesture, but this is very risky… we're going to have to be very careful."

"I know, stop panicking," I groused. "You worry too much."

"Well one of us has to!" he replied, crossly. "What time tomorrow morning?"

I looked up at the sky. It was getting later.

"I think we should have our lunch before we go tomorrow," I said. "Otherwise we're going to be starving again, so I'll have breakfast at 9 o'clock and meet you about 9:30 and start making plans, then we can go through the magic door for around 1 o'clock, after we've had something to eat. What do you think?"

"Yeah, sounds like a plan to me!"

We decided to make travelling through the magic door a 1 o'clock thing every day. That way, each day we'd know where we were and what time it was back home without getting confused.

When I got home, my mum and dad were sitting in the living room, watching the TV.

"Hello George!" Dad called.

"Have you had a good day?" Mum asked.

"Yes," I said, "but we've just been around Paul's house and his grandma just died."

At once, they turned down the TV.

"I'm really sorry to hear that," said Mum.

Dad asked, "Is he okay?"

"Yes," I said. "Well, not really, but he's going to be fine. Me and Thomas will look after him."

"You're a good boy," Mum said.

I nodded and offered her a smile, but all the time I was thinking if she knew the half of it, she wouldn't be saying that.

I sat on the rug, glancing at the TV. "Mum, Dad, can I ask about what you used to get up to when you were little?"

"Well, the normal things, really," Mum said. "I grew up down south in the city, but your dad grew up here."

"Where did you live, dad?" I asked.

"I've lived in this village all my life," he replied. "I grew up just around the corner, in my grandma and grandad's old house. Your grandma grew up there, too."

I know, I thought. *I was just there!*

"What were your grandma and grandad like?" I asked him, as they had died before I was born.

Dad smiled, remembering them. "My grandma always used to spoil me, but my grandad used to talk to me like I was an adult. He could be a little abrupt, but that's how I think they all were in those days. Men were expected to grow up quickly." He sighed. "I know he cared, but really all I saw was just a miserable old man who cared more about his dog than anything else."

"That's horrible," said Mum.

"What kind of dog did he have?" I asked. I had a feeling that I'd met him, too.

"A black Labrador, I believe," he said. "He always had black Labs. The one I knew was called Rex."

"Did you get into trouble a lot?" I asked.

Dad laughed. "About as much as you and your brothers do. I was always coming home with cuts and scrapes, or mucky clothes. I used to play at the quarry before my friend died. I was always getting into mischief and doing things I shouldn't be doing, like climbing trees or making rafts for the quarry."

"How do you make a raft?" I asked, interested.

"Easy," he said, pleased about my enthusiasm. "I used to get four spare car wheels and strap them under a door with rope. That's how you make a raft!" He grinned. "It was a lot of fun, but not terribly safe!"

"Who taught you how to build one?" I asked him. I couldn't imagine my other grandad doing that.

"My dad's best mate. When we were your age we'd play on the quarry pool all day." He frowned. "But this is no good to you because you're not allowed down the quarry, and if I ever find out you've been down there you'll be grounded for the rest of the summer holidays."

"I know, Dad," I said, thinking quickly. Paul's holiday came to mind. "I was only thinking it would be cool to make one, one day. Maybe we could go camping and you could teach me."

Dad looked delighted. "I'll see what we can do. But you have to promise me not to play at the quarry, George."

"I promise," I said, but I had my fingers crossed behind my back.

CHAPTER ELEVEN

OUR NEW DEN

The next morning came and again I woke early, but this time I decided to have a lie-in as we weren't planning on going through the magic door until the afternoon.

After a while, Mum popped her head through the door and asked if I was OK.

"Yes Mum," I replied, sleepily. "Just having a lie-in."

"I wished you'd have said," she complained. "I've made your breakfast and it's gone cold. You're normally up by now."

I felt a little bad, but I couldn't tell her that I was tired because I was a time traveller and out for 20 hours a day. I thought about staying in bed for a little longer, but as I lay there I found I couldn't rest. I was so excited I needed to get up.

Eating my cold breakfast, I started asking my mum questions in the hope that I could learn as much about the past as possible.

"Did you know my great grandma and grandad?" I asked.

"Yes," she said. "Your dad and I would go around there for tea twice a week before they died."

"Was Great Grandad really as grumpy as Dad said?"

"Oh, yes! Yes he was," she replied. "But your great grandma was lovely. Once his grandma died, we stopped going around to see your grandad as often! He was more interested in that dog of his."

He sounded like a right grumpy old man, I thought to myself. So grumpy in fact that, many years later, neither Mum nor Dad could think of anything nice to say about him.

After breakfast, I went out. "I'm off out now, Mum. See you at lunchtime."

I went over to Thomas's house, but his curtains were shut and I didn't want to knock the door and wake his dog up. So, instead, I went down to see if Paul was up. His curtains were open.

I knocked on his door and his mum answered. "Morning George," she said with a sad look on her face.

"Good morning," I said. "I'm sorry to hear about Paul's grandma."

"Thank you," she said. "Paul is getting his shoes on, he'll be out in a minute. Would you like to come in and wait?"

"No, that's okay," I said. "I'll wait outside."

I shifted awkwardly from one foot to another. The truth was, I didn't know what to say to his mum. A few minutes later Paul came out of the house with a huge grin on his face.

"It's been really hard pretending to be sad," I said. "But obviously I can't tell them why I'm so happy. When I went to bed last night I slept with a grin on my face. I'm so excited to meet my grandma again! I can't believe I have to wait until I get back from my holidays."

I told him we needed to call on Thomas, but his curtains were closed.

"I'll go," Paul offered. "His mum won't tell me off because my grandma's just died. She'll feel sorry for me!" He laughed.

"Shh! If anybody heard us, they'd think we were being disrespectful," I said.

"I know," he replied. "I should try and be a little bit more upset."

As we expected the dog went mad, barking and scratching at the door, and about a minute later Thomas's mum threw the door open. Before she could start shouting, however, she realised it was Paul and said, "Oh, hello Paul. I was sorry to hear about your grandma."

"Thank you," he said. "I'm sorry if it's too early, I just couldn't sleep and was wondering if Thomas wanted to come out?"

"Of course," she smiled. "I'll go and see if he's up. Would you and George like to come in and wait?"

"No, that's okay, thanks," he said. "We'll just wait out here for him."

We grabbed the ball out of Thomas's yard and started kicking it around the road until Thomas came out. He had Patch with him.

"Morning sleepyhead," I said.

"Well, to be fair George, you did say we weren't going out until after 9:30!"

"I couldn't sleep," I said. "I've been too excited."

"So what time are we going through the magic door?" Paul asked.

"1 o'clock," I said.

Thomas and I explained what we'd decided about eating lunch before going through so we wouldn't get too hungry.

"We really could do with getting some money from the past so that we've got some way of buying food when we're there," Thomas said.

"I've got an idea," I replied. "Why don't I go ask my grandma and grandad if they've got any old money from the past? Grandad is a bit of a hoarder, he's bound to have something kicking about."

"That's a good idea," said Paul.

"Yeah, let's do that," Thomas agreed.

Grandma was coming out of the house as we arrived.

"Morning boys," she said. "Sorry to hear about your grandma, Paul. She was a good friend back in the day."

"Did you know my grandma?" he asked.

"Yes," she said. "We used to play together when we were children."

"Really?" Paul asked, transfixed.

"Oh yes," said Grandma. "She lived over in Ash Meadows, but we'd both go over and play out in the park at the end of her village with our friends."

Thomas, Paul and I shared a look. Now we knew where we could find her.

"I'll try and find out as much as I can about your grandma and grandad from my grandma and grandad later on, Paul!" I whispered, as Grandma put some rubbish in the bin.

"Thanks," he said. "But my grandad was never in my grandma's life for long. I think he died before I was born, but I don't know what happened."

"What can I do for you boys, then?" she asked. "To what do I owe the honour?"

"We wanted to ask if you and Grandad had any money from the past, because we're playing a game and we need some old pennies," I said.

Just then, Grandad came to the door. "Hello trouble." He laughed and ruffled my hair. "What was that I heard? You were after some old pennies?"

"Yes, Grandad, we just wanted to know if you had any old money from when you were little?"

He glanced at the three of us. "As it happens, I do have a tin of old pennies and shillings and suchlike. Come in, boys, and let's have a look! Patch can come in, too - I have some treats for him."

Grandma shook her head, fondly, and gave Patch a fuss.

As we went into the kitchen, Grandad reached up and grabbed an old biscuit tin that rattled and sounded heavy as he put it down on the table.

"Have a look through there, boys. I'm sure you'll find everything you'll need," he said as he bent down to stroke the dog.

"Do you mind if I give Patch a treat?" Grandad asked Thomas.

"No, that's fine, he likes treats," said Thomas. "And he loves you."

"I have some bacon flavoured treats here," Grandad said, "I bet they're his favourite?"

"Yes," Thomas said, smiling. "He goes mad for them."

As we eagerly sifted through the tin, we noticed that there were quite a lot of pennies and shilling coins. The kind that we don't use anymore.

"Are these all from when you were a little boy, Grandad?" I asked.

He looked inside the tin and said, "Everything in the tin you could spend while I was a little boy - and even up to when I was a young man. You can have them all if you like."

"What, all of them, Grandad?" I asked, stunned.

"Yes! They're no good to me anymore. You might as well play with them." He smiled at us. "You might as well keep the biscuit tin as well. You can hide it in the vault with your clothes, so when you're playing the game everything is together."

Good idea, I thought. "Thank you, Grandad," I said aloud.

"Yes, thanks very much," Thomas said as we put the coins back in the tin.

We collected Patch - who seemed a little disappointed to be leaving behind the bacon-flavoured treats - and set off.

"Bye, Grandma! Bye, Grandad!" I called, over my shoulder.

"Your grandad is really cool, George!" Thomas said.

"Yeah," said Paul. "Really, if you think about it, he never hassles us, or questions us. He just gives us cool stuff to play with."

"Let's go down to the oak tree and put this tin in the vault," I suggested. "Then we can play for a bit before coming back down after lunch."

"Okay," they both said.

After a short while - maybe half an hour or so - when we'd played on the rope swing for a bit, we decided to make our way back home to get something to eat.

As we got into the village, Paul's mum was talking to one of the neighbours out in the backyard. "Hello boys," she said. "Paul, we're going down to see your auntie and uncle, so we can make arrangements for your grandma's funeral. You need to come with us."

Our faces fell. Paul's auntie and uncle lived quite far away, which meant they'd probably be staying there for a few days.

"Can't I stay here?" Paul asked his mum.

"No," she said. "You haven't seen your auntie or uncle in a long time, and I want you with me."

"Okay then, Mum," he said sadly.

Dismayed, the three of us gravitated towards Thomas's house.

"What are we going to do?" Paul asked. "I know I wasn't going to see my grandma until after my holiday, but I was hoping to find out where she lived at least."

"Leave it with me," I said. "Thomas and I can go and find out where she lived and who else she used to play with. We can ask my grandma."

"I suppose I could find out more about her from Mum and my aunt and uncle," he said. "So, that's not a bad thing."

Thomas said that we still didn't know her name back then.

"Yes we do! I asked my mum last night," he told us, grinning. "She was called Elsa Jones."

Paul's mum came and got him. As they walked away, I heard Paul begin to interrogate her about his grandma.

After lunch, Thomas and I met outside my house. It was about half past 12.

"Let's go down and get changed," I said. "And maybe we can take some money to buy some food or sweets when we get there."

"Yes," he said, "let's do that!"

We went off to the quarry full of excitement. Every trip through the magic door was exciting, but with Paul's request it felt like we had a proper mission to complete.

As we walked towards the water, we talked about how we were going to find Paul's grandma; the village where she grew up was a good hour's walk away.

"Why don't we take our bikes?" Thomas suggested. "That will be quicker."

"No," I said. "We can't take ours - they're too modern. Actually, that's not a bad idea, though!"

"What?" he said, puzzled. "You just said we can't take our bikes because they're too modern!"

"No, we can't," I said. "But we could try to borrow some in the past. That way we could ride over to the village in about 30 minutes, which would give us more time to try and find Elsa."

"Okay," he said, "but where do we start? Where would we find two bikes in 1936?"

"Well," I replied, "we haven't seen the girls playing on bikes, so we have to assume they don't own any. I think we saw a second-hand shop in the town, though, so maybe if we go in there we can buy two."

Thomas looked dubious. "Let's say they do have two bikes, how are we going to pay for them?"

"The money Grandad gave us," I replied. "There should be enough to buy two second-hand bikes. If you think about it, you could probably buy a second-hand bike in 1936 for a few shillings or something? I don't know, but we could take it with us and try."

"Let's go through the magic door and walk down to town straight away," I added.

"We might have to be careful, though," Thomas reminded me. "If we go down at 1 o'clock, people will think we're playing truant, and we don't want the school board, the police, or that grumpy old man looking for us."

We give it some thought, then came up with the idea to tell people we came from the village where Elsa lived and that the school is closed because of a burst water pipe.

"Sounds like a plan," I said. "We'll do that."

The weather on the far side of the door was dark and cloudy.

"I don't like the look of this weather," Thomas remarked, eyeing it warily.

"I know," I said. "We don't have coats. People will think we're mad if it pours down and we're out here without them."

Up until now we'd assumed the weather would always be the same on both sides of the door.

Thomas said, "Maybe we need a wooden box this side of the door, so that we can hide things like coats and bikes for when we come over."

"Bikes?" I said, with a laugh. "What kind of box are you thinking of?"

"Well then, maybe we can find an old shed or something?"

"Okay," I said, nodding. "An old disused shed is a good idea. We should try to find one first, and then by the time we get into town it will be past 3 p.m. and the schools will be out."

"That's a good point," he said. "It means no one will ask us any awkward questions and we won't have to lie about what we're doing there."

"What about the allotments at the end of the village?" I suggested. "Assuming they're still there in this time, we could hire an allotment with a shed on it."

We went to have a look, but the allotments were all smart and new, not like in our time.

"I'm not sure we'll find an empty spare shed here," Thomas said dubiously. "They all look new."

I thought he had a point. "Well, we can go and have a look anyway," I replied.

As we walked along the footpath in between the allotments, a man looked up from weeding a vegetable patch and asked, "What are you boys looking for?"

I gave him a smile and - thinking quickly - I said, "My uncle's asked us to come down and see if there are any allotments free."

"As a matter of fact, you're in luck," the man replied. "The one on the corner, by the woods, just came free this morning. Is your uncle going to come down and have a look at it?"

Thomas and I looked at each other. This was perfect.

"He's busy today, but we could look instead, if that's okay?"

Dusting soil from his hands, the man showed us around the allotment, pointing out the beds for vegetables, a small garden shed, and a greenhouse with old, empty, dusty shelves in it. There were also some old tools, gardening gloves, and a scruffy old pair of yellow wellies under the bench in the allotment.

"This would be perfect for him," I said. "What do we need to do next?"

"Well," the man replied, "it will cost 24 pence per month and you need your uncle to come down and sign the paperwork."

Thomas and I looked at each other. I bit my lip.

"Is this a problem?" the man asked, suspicious.

"Not a big problem," I said to the man. "Erm, it's just we wanted to do this as a surprise for our uncle, for his birthday next week. Is there any way that we could take it on now, without him knowing? We'd like to get it all tidied up for him."

The man stood and pondered for minute or two, before replying, "That's a nice thing to do, but where are two boys like you going to find the money? I'd need at least three months in advance."

"Our mum has been saving up for him," Thomas said quickly. "That's..." He counted up on his fingers. "72 pence, right? We've got enough."

"Alright," he said. "I'll need your uncle to come down in a week to fill in the paperwork."

"That's great," I said to the man, shaking his hand and pulling out a pocketful of change.

"You shouldn't be walking around with that kind of cash on you," he remarked, looking at me. "Could you imagine if you lost it? You'd be in so much trouble with your mum!"

"Um, yes," I said. Neither Thomas nor I could believe what we were hearing. There was such a big difference between the value of money in the two different times. "We're careful, though. Mum trusts us."

Nodding, the man said, "You'd better be." He pulled out a key from his pocket and added, "There you go, boys. Have fun and look after it, and remember your uncle needs to be here this time next week to sign for it, or I'll need the keys back from you."

"We'll make sure he knows," I said as we walked down towards the shed to have a look at our new hideout.

As the man walked away, I said to Thomas, "We need to be careful about the amount of money we carry. Luckily, that man didn't ask too many questions, but if we pull the equivalent of £30 out in town, people are going to think we're thieves or something."

"Never mind that," Thomas replied, "what are we going to do in a week when we need your uncle to come and sign for it?"

"We'll cross that bridge when we come to it," I said. "We need to pay attention and double check everything we do, or we'll end up breaking our own laws."

Just as we got inside our shed, the skies opened up and it poured down with rain.

"That was good timing! We'll stay nice and dry in here," I said, with a grin on my face.

"Yes," he agreed. "This will make a great hideout for when we're here."

We looked at each other and grinned even more. It was only an allotment, but to us it felt like we'd just got our first ever home. As the rain came down outside, we started planning what we were going to do with the shed.

"We should call it 'The Den'," I said.

"Okay, 'The Den' it is," he replied.

There was already a little stove in the corner, with a chimney poking through the roof.

"I can't see us using this through the summer holidays," I said to Thomas, examining it.

There was also a long wooden bench that reached right across the back wall. It looked like it was made to hold plant pots. There were some old tools on it that were probably left behind by the previous person and two sections of tree trunk that had been cut down and made into stools.

"Okay," I said, taking a seat. "Let's get serious and work out how much money we should carry on us, and what we're willing to pay for old second-hand bikes. We'll need to get our story straight as to where we got it from, should anybody ask."

"We could tell people that we've earned the money doing odd jobs and that we've saved up," Thomas suggested.

"Okay," I replied. "That seems believable, but how much does a second-hand bike cost?"

"Well," he said, "I know that an allotment costs around about £10 per month to rent back home and over here it's 24p."

"So, if we say 24p here is £10 back home, that should give us an idea as to what things cost and how much we should be carrying around with us."

I carried on, "If this is the case, we should never have more than £5 on us - or should I say, 12 pence - so as not to raise suspicion. I also think we should go back home and grab the biscuit tin full of money and leave it here. Particularly with David and Sean hanging around."

"We could," he said, "but if we do, we'd need to bury it in case anybody came to the allotment and found it."

"Okay," I agreed. "Let's do that tomorrow. How much do you have on you?" he asked.

We both turned out our pockets and, after having paid the 72p for the three months' allotment rent, we still had £2 between us.

This was far too much money so we put £1.50 under the ash in the stove and took 25p each, intending to go into the town to see if we could buy a bike each from the second-hand shop.

We didn't have long to wait for the rain to stop.

"We need to see if we can find a lock for the shed and maybe a lock box for the money tin when we're in town," I said.

We left the allotment, locking the gate behind us and heading towards the town.

"We need to try and avoid bumping into the girls, too," I said. "We don't want them asking too many questions as to where we got the money from, particularly as we told them our parents didn't have much."

"I thought we were going tell people we earned it through odd jobs?" Thomas asked.

"Yes," I said, "but I don't like lying to them, so the fewer questions they ask, the better."

"Lying to them! Are you kidding me?" he asked. "Every word that comes out of our mouths is a lie - every time we speak to them we have to make something up."

"I suppose you're right, when you put it like that, but nonetheless we need to avoid them for today," I said. "We've got to try and find out as much as we can about Paul's grandma."

We set off and made our way towards the town, proud of the plans we'd made. By now we were approaching the town and it was getting on towards 2:30 p.m. The town was busy, full of people going about their day-to-day business.

"Where was that second-hand shop?" Thomas asked.

"Just next door to the butchers, down the far end of town."

"Should we jump on the tram?" he asked.

"Yes, why not?" I replied. "It sounds like fun! I wonder how much it is?"

Just then, the tram pulled up beside us.

"Excuse me, sir," I said to the conductor, "how much is a tram ride for two of us to the other end of town?"

"The other end of town!" He laughed. "Two young boys like you should be running down there at your age! Halfpenny each!"

Thomas said, "So, that's a penny for the two of us."

"Is it?" I said snarkily. "I didn't realise two halfpennies made a whole penny."

"Well, are you two getting on then?" the conductor asked as Paul scowled at me. "We're about to pull away."

We both nearly tripped over each other trying to get on. Thomas handed the conductor one penny.

"Let's go and sit upstairs," I said, already halfway up them.

We ran to the very back and sat down.

The tram was electric powered, with an aerial running to overhead lines. The seats were made of hard wooden beams with a tiny amount of padding on them. The whole thing smelled of real leather and wood, and the sweat of the passengers. There were shiny brass handles to hold onto.

This was so exciting! We weren't even allowed on a bus on our own back at home. We felt so grown up! We were travelling on a tram and we had our own allotment!

"Could this be any better?" Thomas asked, and I shook my head happily.

We were only on the tram for a minute before it screeched to a rattling halt.

"Last stop, end of the line!" the conductor shouted to all of the passengers.

"That was a short trip," I said to Thomas.

"What do you expect for a penny?" He laughed. "Come on then, let's go to the second-hand shop and see what we can find. But this time, try not to get yourself run over! How would we explain that to your mum?"

"There," I pointed. "It's called 'Seconds to Go'."

Outside the shop there were all sorts of second-hand things on a table in front of the window. We stopped to look at all of the junk on the table and the shopkeeper came out and asked, "Anything I can help you with, boys?"

"Yes," I replied, "we're looking for a bike each."

"You mean bicycles?" the man asked.

"Yes, sir," I said quickly. "Sorry, yes. Bicycles!"

He turned away for a moment and I rolled my eyes at Thomas.

"We have several in the back of the shop," he told us. "Come in and have a look."

We followed the shopkeeper into his shop.

As he pushed the door open we heard the bell rattle. I looked up; it was a brass bell, hanging on a coiled piece of metal that caught the door each time it opened. When we walked in the floor was dirty and dusty. The smell throughout the whole shop was one of damp wood and mouldy clothes.

This didn't put us off wanting to stay in there and look around, though - the shop was like something out of a museum. It was packed with all sorts of stuff, stacked haphazardly in piles that reached right to the ceiling. There were all sorts of things, from garden tools to clothes and shoes, to home appliances.

We couldn't help ourselves; we just kept picking things up to examine them and putting them back down before moving onto the next.

"Here we go, boys!" the shopkeeper called, from the back of the shop.

As we made our way towards the back of the shop, by the counter, he pulled forward one of two old bikes.

"Will these do?" he asked.

Thomas and I glanced at each other and asked if we could have a minute to look at them.

"Yes," he replied, "but be careful." He walked out of the door to speak to more potential customers looking at the junk on the table outside.

I looked at Thomas and asked, "What on Earth are these?"

He laughed. "I know! The seats are real leather - and where are the brakes? How do we stop them?"

"Look at the tyres," I laughed. "They're just solid rubber! This will rattle our teeth!"

"Well, at least they have springs under the seat," Thomas observed.

"I suppose so."

We were looking for a price tag to see how much they were, but we couldn't find one.

Just then the shopkeeper came back in, shaking his head and muttering, "Some people want everything for nothing.

Have you made up your minds?" he asked us both. "Would you like to buy them?"

"That depends," I said. "How much for both of them?"

The man rubbed his chin, looking up in the air as if he didn't know the price and said, "28p each, but if you buy them both you can have them for 50p."

"Bargain buy," I said to Thomas, out of the side of my mouth and under my breath.

"Okay, sir," Thomas replied. "We'll take them. Just one question, though - how do we stop them?"

"What do you mean, how do you stop them?" He chuckled. "You have feet, don't you?"

"I think you're supposed to put your feet on the ground to stop yourself, Thomas," I said.

"We'd better come back and buy some shoes tomorrow then," he joked. "We'll wear these ones out straightaway."

We paid the man, pushed the bikes out of the shop, climbed on them, and started riding them home along the road through the centre of the town. We were rattling and shaking about, making funny noises through our mouths as we shook across the cobblestones.

"This is brilliant!" I said to Thomas.

"I know," he said, "I still can't believe we're doing this! This is so much fun!"

As we started to make our way towards the village we saw the girls walking towards us.

"Hello, boys," they said, as we tried to stop the bikes with our feet, and Thomas fell off his.

"Where did you get those from?" Aly asked.

"We just bought them from the second-hand shop in town."

"How much did you pay for them?" Iris asked.

We told them that we got a bargain price of 50 pence for both at the second-hand shop.

All three of them laughed. "He saw you coming, didn't he?"

We didn't care as we were in a good mood and happy with our new bikes and allotment.

"Where are you off to now?" Em asked.

"We're off to our allotment," I said proudly. "It's the one down by the woods, the end one."

"Aren't you too young to have an allotment?" Em asked.

"We," I replied. "We say *our* allotment but it is in fact my uncle's, and he's asked us to tidy it up for him while he's away on holiday."

"Quick thinking," Thomas said, under his breath. "That was close!"

"Are you going down there today?" Aly asked.

"Maybe," I said. "Why? Do you want to see it?"

"Of course," they all replied together, excited.

I think they were excited to have somewhere else other than home to go and play, should it rain. As we got to the allotments and I started to unlock the gate, I looked at Thomas and said, "We forgot to buy a lock for the shed."

"Why would you need a lock for the shed?" Iris asked. "What are you going to put in the shed that you'd need to lock it for?"

"The bikes," I explained. "We need to lock our bikes away in the shed."

"Why don't you just take them home?" Aly asked.

"What's with all the questions, are you the police?" Thomas asked, laughing.

"Alright," said Em, "we were only playing with you."

When we got to the shed, the first thing Aly said was, "This is a bit scruffy! It could do with a woman's touch."

Straightaway, me and Thomas looked at each other.

Typical, I thought. *Bring a girl to a boy's den and they try and change it.*

"This is our uncle's shed," Thomas said quickly. "We're only allowed to come down to tidy it up. It's not somewhere we can come all the time."

"Well, it's scruffy, anyway," Em said. "Why would we want to spend lots of time down here?"

"What are you both doing for the rest of the day?" Iris asked.

Straightaway, Thomas replied, "Nothing, we've got nothing planned."

I looked at him, confused. "Actually, we're supposed to be going over to see Paul's grandma."

"That's okay," Iris said. "We'll just go down and play on the rope swing and catch up with you later."

"Why did you say that to them?" Thomas asked, when they'd gone. "You know I like Iris."

"Oh, stop saying that!" I said. "That's my grandma you're talking about."

"I know, but she's a nice person and I'd like to be her friend," he said.

"Well, that's fair enough, but we shouldn't' get side-tracked," I told him. "We bought those bikes so we could ride over and find out where Paul's grandma lives."

"Yes, you're right," he said. "Let's go, then - and when we come back, if we have time, we can play down the rope swing with them. If that's okay?"

"Yeah, alright."

"What time is it now, George?" Thomas asked.

"It's just coming up to half past 4."

We worked out that we needed to leave the past at 9 o'clock that night at the latest in order to get home in time for tea. That gave us about 3 and a half hours to get over to Paul's grandma's village, Ash Meadows.

Chapter Twelve

Tracking Paul's Grandma

We set off on our bikes towards the village where we thought Paul's grandma lived, but when we got to the end of the road where we'd normally turn right to get to her village, everything looked different. There was no road, only a dusty old track made up of stone and gravel.

"Where's the road?" Thomas asked.

I shrugged. "I guess it just hasn't been built yet."

"This day just keeps getting better and better," he said drily.

Riding uncomfortable bikes over uneven ground took a toll, and we arrived at Ash Meadows village almost one hour after we left.

"Where do we start?" Thomas asked.

"Over there in the village shop," I suggested. "Let's go in and ask the shopkeeper if they know who Elsa Jones is."

"Okay, but before we go in, do you have any more change on you?"

I knew why he was asking. My stomach rumbled. It felt like a long time since lunch.

"Yes," I said, checking in my pocket.

"Good, I'm hungry," said Thomas. "I think we should get some sweets or crisps, or something, and a drink."

"We have about 11p left over," I told him. "That's about £2 back home, so it should be enough."

As we went in, we heard the now-familiar ding-a-ling of the bell above the door. I supposed all shops had a similar type of bell. The first thing I noticed was the sweet smell of chocolate and sugary treats. My stomach rumbled again.

Although the floor was made of wood it was far cleaner than any of the shops we'd been in up until now.

Across the whole back wall of the shop were sweets of all different types, and through the back we could see a man in an apron pouring a hot, sticky liquid onto a tray. Interested, I craned to look.

"Excuse me, Miss!" I said to the lady behind the counter. "What's that man doing over there?"

The woman behind the counter smiled. "He's making hard-boiled sweets. Would you like to watch?"

"Yes, please," we both replied at once.

"Come along, then," she said kindly.

Thomas and I followed her through to the back and watched the man pouring a glue-like liquid into a tray full of holes shaped like lemons. It smelled amazing - and we could feel the heat even as far back as we were standing.

"What's he making?" I asked the lady.

"Lemon drops!" she replied. "They're new and very popular, would you like to try one?"

We didn't need to be asked twice. The lemon drops were sweet and fresh, and very tasty.

"You're not from around here, are you, boys?" the woman asked as she ushered us back into the shop. "I don't recognise you and I know everybody in the village."

"No, we're from Meadow View!" I said.

"Meadow View," she replied, raising her eyebrow. "That's a long way to come."

"Yes, but we're looking for my friend's cousin," I said. "You might know her. Her name's Elsa Jones."

The lady looked up, rubbing her chin. "Elsa Jones! Yes, I know her mother. They live down at the end of the village, by the old church."

"Thank you," I said, pleased with our progress.

"Would you like to buy any lemon drops?" she asked. "Halfpenny per ounce."

We bought ourselves an ounce of lemon drops and a bottle of lemonade each, all of which cost threepence and a halfpenny.

We thanked the woman and went back outside to our bicycles, carrying our bounty. Thomas held his bottle of lemonade up to the light.

"What a strange colour," he said. "It looks like honey, only watery."

"Well, it must be okay to drink," I said.

We both took a drink and it was delicious.

"Wow, this actually tastes like real lemons! It's absolutely lovely," he said.

I agreed. It lacked the bitterness of the lemonade we were used to.

Thomas put a lemon drop in his mouth, savouring the taste. "Mmm, these are lovely, too," he said. "I could get used to these!"

We finished our drinks and put the bottles in the bin outside the shop, then we put the sweets in our pockets and made our way towards the end of the village, where the church tower rose high above the houses.

Next to the church, there was one house on its own.

"That must be it," I said to Thomas.

As we approached the gate, the door opened and for some reason we ducked down behind the wall. I don't know why; we hadn't done anything wrong. Perhaps it was instinct.

We heard someone walking up the path towards the gate.

From the house, a woman shouted, "Elsa! Where are you going?"

"I'm off to the shop to buy some sweets," a girl's voice replied.

"Alright, then. Don't be long!"

From our hiding place we watched the girl come out of the gate and walk off up the village, towards the shop.

"Well, now we know who Elsa is and what she looks like," I said. "I think that's enough for today. I suppose it's time we went home."

We jumped on our bikes. As we approached Elsa, I rang my bell. She turned around and looked straight at me and smiled.

"Nice bicycles, boys!" she said, giggling.

"That's the second time today somebody's laughed at our bikes!" I said, with a laugh, and we rode off out of the village and headed back to our new den.

By the time we reached it, it was getting late. We needed to lock our bikes away in the den and get back to the magic door. The girls would have headed home long before we returned, to Thomas's irritation.

At this time of night there was no one around the quarry, but as we made our way towards the magic door I caught a glimpse of the young boy I kept seeing.

As I turned around to tell Thomas, he said, "Yes! I saw him too, but only for a second. Who do you think he is and, more to the point, *when* do you think he is?"

As we walked closer, the boy disappeared.

"Do you think there's another magic door?" Thomas asked me.

"It's possible, I suppose, but if there *is* another magic door, where does it go?" I replied, thoughtfully.

We walked through our magic door, making sure we were crouching down in the grass where no one could see us on the other side.

"Coast's clear," I said. "Let's go down and get changed."

"We could have a look tomorrow and see if we can find out whether or not there's another magic door, and how to get through it," Thomas proposed.

"Okay," I replied, "but we could do with Paul being with us as we might need to split up and be in three different places at once."

"True, but that breaks one of the laws," he reminded me. "'Always stick together'."

"We'll be careful," I assured him.

"We'd better get home in time for tea," he said.

Walking home, we both looked over at the allotment where our den was.

I looked at Thomas and said, "I wonder how long our den has been gone?"

"I know," he said, "the whole area just looks so scruffy."

The allotments, which were once in pristine condition, now looked terrible, with bric-a-brac fence panels and barbed wire everywhere, and sheds that had almost collapsed with ripped roof felts and broken windows.

Forgetting the allotments, I said, "If there *is* another magic door we need to try and work out where it is. We could even draw on our map where we think it could be."

As we turned onto our road, I heard my mum call, "George! Come on, it's time for tea!"

"Can I come back out after tea?" I asked, as we got to the end of our garden.

"No," she replied. "You have to help me tidy up your bedroom, ready for decorating."

I told Thomas that I'd better go. "I'll see you tomorrow morning - 9 o'clock."

"See you!"

Chapter Thirteen

Discovering Another Magic Door

At 8:30 a.m. the next morning I left the house and started making my way towards Thomas's, though it was an hour earlier than we'd agreed. On the way there, I noticed Paul's mum's car still wasn't there. When I got to Thomas's he came out the house with Patch and waved.

"I don't think Paul's home!" I said. "His mum's car isn't there."

"He's not," Thomas replied, "I've already knocked on him this morning."

I looked down at Patch and asked, "How long do you have the dog for?"

"My mum says I have to have him out until lunchtime."

"He might be able to help us find another magic door," I said. "Remember the last time we took him through? He went mad."

Thomas agreed. "Then we need to grab the map and a pencil and mark off where the dog reacts."

He went back inside for a pencil before coming back out again, then we made our way to the oak tree to collect the map.

"Okay then, Thomas," I said, "how are we going to do this?"

"Well," he replied, "we should stand in front of our magic door and watch Patch's reaction, then move the dog around the quarry slowly to see if he can find another."

"Sounds like a plan to me. Let's do it!"

Sure enough, as we approached the magic door, the dog started to bark and pull away.

"Where do you think the other one might be?" I asked, giving Patch a comforting pat.

"Over there," Thomas pointed. "To the right of the door near the quarry wall."

Slowly, we made a circuit of the quarry pool, but nothing happened. The dog never so much as whimpered. He simply bounced along through the grass, quite contentedly. Returning to our original position, far enough from our magic door for Patch to remain calm, we sat down in the grass, looking at the map and across the water.

Rather at a loss, we decided while we were there that we'd start throwing stones into the middle and seeing who could get the furthest and make the biggest splash.

Thomas threw his stone as hard as he could and it landed almost in the middle of the quarry, by the wall.

"Beat that!" he said, triumphant.

I picked up a stone about the size of the palm of my hand, pulled my arm back as far as I could, and then threw it as hard as I could.

We watched it fly through the air, waiting to see where it would splash into the water, but it never landed. It simply slipped out of sight in mid-air.

"Did you hit the quarry wall?" Thomas asked.

"No, I don't think so," I said, frowning.

Thomas pulled a face. "Well, I didn't hear a splash in the water."

"Me neither," I said.

"Throw another one!" he suggested.

I told him to throw another first, as we needed to do it the same as we did before for scientific integrity. So, Thomas grabbed a rock that filled his hand and threw it as hard and as far as he could. Again, it landed in middle of the quarry by the wall, making a big splash.

"Now, your turn!" he said as he handed me another rock of a similar size.

I pulled my arm back, but just as I was about to throw it, another rock came flying towards us. It landed on the ground at our feet with a thud. Looking at it, my mouth fell open in surprise. It wasn't just any rock, but the one I'd thrown before. Patch barked at it, uncertain, and tried to pull away from the spot where we were standing.

I dropped the stone in my hand and we both ran off, the dog pulling us away.

Around about 25 metres away from where we were throwing the stones we stopped and started laughing.

"Well, I think we found the second magic door," Thomas said, through his giggles.

"Yes, I know," I replied, still laughing. "I wonder who threw it back."

"I don't know," Thomas said. "It must have upset them, for them to throw it back!"

"I think it would probably scare the life out of me, seeing a rock flying through the air from nowhere," I admitted. "If we weren't already time travellers, that is. "There's probably somebody on the other side of the door thinking that someone's hiding and throwing stones at them."

Based on where the stone had vanished and then reappeared from, we were able to work out that the second magic door was just over the water by the wall, so we quickly jotted it down on the map and called it 'Door 2'.

"The one thing we can be sure of," I observed, "is that we can see the magic door from both sides, because each time we both saw that boy, we were on the other side of the door and now we've seen the stone disappear from this side. What do you think?"

"I don't know," Thomas replied, "do you think there's any more magic doors across the water?"

I looked at him and smiled. "There's only one way to find out!"

Thomas must have been thinking the same as me, as he grinned and passed me a rock I hadn't asked for.

"Go on, then," he said. "You throw farther. Throw it as far as you can, but 10 feet to the right of the new magic door, where you threw the last one."

I drew my arm right back, as far as I could, and threw the rock with all my strength. It splashed into the water with something of an anti-climax.

"Well, there's not one there," he remarked. "Try another."

"Okay, but pass me a smaller one," I requested. "It's starting to make my arm hurt. Plus, if there *is* anybody on the other side, we don't want a big rock like that. We might hurt them."

After hurling a few more stones we decided that there were no more magic doors - at least not over the water where we were looking.

We were contemplating what to do next when we heard a voice behind us, making both of us jump out of our skin.

It was David. "What are two doing down here? You know you're not supposed to be down here; Dad's going to kill you when he finds out!" he said, with some glee.

"Don't tell," I begged. "Please."

His face cracked into a grin. "You know the deal. Sean and me are going down town, and if anybody asks, you two have been with us all day down at the rope swing!"

"Right," I said, as David wandered off, presumably to meet up with Sean.

"I wish he wouldn't sneak up like that," I said. "I felt my life pass before my eyes. Come on, Thomas. Let's go down to the rope swing until those two clear off!"

Playing on the swing as Patch splashed about in the stream, we spoke about the possibility of a third door and where it would likely be. There was no way of telling where it could be - if there even was one - or where and when it might lead.

Later, when we were sure my brothers had gone, we changed our clothes and took the tin of money out of the vault Grandad had made for us.

Once we were through the magic door, I said, "Let's go up then and hide our money in our den."

As we started walking towards the allotments, we saw Aly and Iris standing at the gate, rattling the padlock and looking over at the den.

While we were watching, Iris called, "Are you there?"

"There they are," Aly said, spotting us.

"Still no Paul today?" Iris asked.

"No," I said, "his Grandma died and he's had to go to his family's house with his parents to arrange the funeral."

"Oh no, that's a shame," Aly replied. "Tell him we're thinking about him."

"Whose is the dog?" Iris asked.

Thomas quickly replied, "Mine," with a big grin on his face. I think he was pleased to have something to show off. "His name is Patch."

She knelt down and started rubbing his ears. The dog was really excited and pleased to see her.

"He must really like you," Thomas commented. "He's not normally this friendly around strangers."

"Of course he likes me," she replied, "I'm a likeable person." She looked up at him and grinned; Thomas beamed back like a Cheshire cat.

"I think Iris is in *love*," Aly said.

"I think you might be right." I grinned, as colour rose in Thomas's cheeks.

"Shut up, you two," Thomas said, as Iris scowled at her sister. "You're embarrassing us."

I leaned closer to Thomas and whispered, "But seriously, remember that's my grandma and we can't interfere with the past, yeah?"

"I know," he muttered. "It's not me who said I'm in love, it was Aly. I like Iris, but that's all. I know that we mustn't break the laws."

"Well, are you going to let us in then?" Aly said.

"Yes, let me open the gate. Hold this, Thomas," I said as I passed him the biscuit tin.

"Give us a biscuit, then," Iris said.

"No, it's not biscuits," I said, without thinking, "it's a little bit of change my grandad gave me so I could buy myself some lunch."

Thomas glared at me.

There was far too much money in the tin for it just to be our lunch money, so we had to try to keep the tin quiet; if the girls heard how much money was in there, they wouldn't believe my quickly created story.

When we got to the den, I opened the door. Thomas and I both tried to get through the gap at the same time and I knocked the tin out of Thomas's hand. All the money spilled onto the floor.

Aly and Iris both gasped.

"What's all that money doing here?" Aly asked, shocked.

"There must be £30 or more!" Iris said, eyes wide.

"You haven't stolen it, have you?" asked Aly.

"No," I said hotly, "I told you, my grandad gave it to me to buy some lunch and other things with."

"Are you two telling us the truth, or are you thieves?" Aly asked, giving us a hard stare.

It was surprisingly intimidating.

"They're not thieves," Iris said, "they're nice boys." She rested her head on Thomas's shoulder and he smiled at her.

"Well, okay," Aly said doubtfully, "but you can't get caught with that amount of money. People will assume you've stolen it. You need to keep it a secret and keep it out of sight."

Agreed, I thought, but before I could reply, my impossibly young grandmother interrupted with a fresh, more troubling question.

"So, if you've got all this money, why are you both riding around with old men's bicycles?" she asked, and both she and Aly giggled. "Are you runaways?"

"Yes," Aly continued, excited. "Have you run away from home? Is this why you're living in a shed and carrying all this money with you?"

"Yes," Thomas replied. "That's it. George is a runaway and he's going to live here, in the den!"

I turned and stared at Thomas, flabbergasted. I couldn't work out what he was thinking. It made us sound very strange indeed, but it was also weirdly plausible, based on when we were. If it stopped the girls asking more questions I was happy to go along with it.

"I knew it," Aly said.

"Yes," Iris replied. "It's the only thing that makes sense."

Thomas told the girls, "You can't tell anybody about George, or that we're here, or the police will come looking for us!"

"Yes," I said slowly, my eyes still on Thomas. "I don't want to go back home. My parents are cruel."

It didn't feel right talking about Mum and Dad like that, even if it was just pretend, but I didn't know what else to say.

"That's alright, we'll keep your secret," Iris promised. "You can trust us. We'll tell our parents that you're from the next village over."

Thomas told them to tell anyone who asked that we were from Ash Meadows.

"Ash Meadows!" Aly gasped. "That's over an hour away."

"Yes, but that's where I'm from," he lied. "That's why we needed the bicycles. At least there's less likelihood of your parents knowing our parents!"

The girls looked at one another for a moment before agreeing.

Iris said, "Yes, alright."

"That sounds like a good idea," agreed Aly.

"So, if you have run away," Iris said, "what about Paul?"

"Paul is actually from Ash Meadows too," I lied, thinking that our stories were getting out of hand and that we'd have to start writing down what we'd said so we could keep our story straight.

We'd have to make sure Paul knew what we'd said, too - and to whom.

My head was spinning a bit, but I just couldn't get the grin off my face. This was the adventure of a lifetime and it showed.

In the den, the girls joined us in planning where we'd hide the money. "Yesterday we put the money under the ash inside the stove," I told them. "There should still be some there from yesterday."

"That won't do," Iris said. "You need to lift up one of the floorboards and put the money in a box, so it's nice and safe."

"That's not a bad idea," I said, impressed.

"We also need to get a lock for the door!" Aly said. "Just in case anyone comes in."

"Then we need to go into town and buy a lock," Iris said.

"Yes, but I think we should walk," Aly suggested, with a grin. "We don't want to be caught out with you on those horrid bicycles."

For the time being, we put all of the money we weren't taking with us under the ash in the stove and stacked some logs on top of it, leaving the biscuit tin on the bench.

As we walked towards town with the girls, we passed the old oak tree.

"That's odd," I said to Thomas, looking up.

"What?" he replied.

"The 'P' you engraved into the tree appears to be more faded than the 'G' and 'T' before it."

"Oh, yeah," he said. "Maybe I didn't cut it as deeply. Remember, I was sitting on your shoulders and my arms were aching."

Up ahead, Aly was looking really happy with herself.

"What's up with you?" I asked. "Why are you smiling like that?"

"No reason," she replied.

I think both she and Iris were really excited to be having their own adventure. After all, they thought I was a runaway in danger of being caught. They were part of a big secret, now - just not quite as big as the truth.

"How do you want to get to town?" I asked them, rattling some change in my pocket. "Shall we travel in style, ladies? Do you want to take the tram?"

"No," Iris said, "kids our age don't have money to spare to use the tram. If we do that, you'll raise suspicion and if anyone sees us they'll tell our mum. She'll think you're thieves and stop us from playing with you both!"

"You're right," I said, a little taken aback. "What can we do with it, then?" I asked, thinking it would be useful to have a gauge of what would and wouldn't be suspicious.

Aly replied, "You can buy sweets and drinks, and the odd little thing, but if you spend too much money in one place people will get suspicious. Or, even worse, try and steal from you."

"The last thing you need is someone following you back to your den and finding out where you keep your money," Iris added.

Good point, I thought.

"Anyway, acting poor won't be difficult for you, wearing those clothes!" Iris laughed.

"Do you think we should get them some more clothes?" Aly asked her sister. "Arthur - our older brother - has grown up and left home, and I'm sure my mother wouldn't have thrown away his old clothes," she added, for our benefit.

Off we walked, towards the town. I walked along with Aly and in front went Thomas and Iris, Iris holding Patch's lead as if he was her new pet.

"Iris has two new friends," I said to Aly.

"Yes, it's strange," she said, with a frown. "Normally, Iris doesn't really like dogs, but she seems to be very fond of that one."

It was a long, steady walk to town from where we were, and took around 30 minutes that afternoon. Along the way, the four of us were laughing and joking and getting along great, as if we'd known each other all our lives.

Which, I supposed, in a weird way, I had.

We were nearly at the town when we reached a small general store, and the girls suggested we go in and get a drink. It was a hot day and all of us were parched.

"Okay," I said, "I am a little thirsty."

"I want an ice cold one," Thomas said.

"Ice cold?" Iris replied. "In the middle of summer? Have you banged your head?"

I shook my head at him and whispered, "Don't be silly, there are no fridges in 1936!"

"Oh yes, I forgot," he said, as the girls peered into the window. "I've also noticed there are no plastic bottles of water, either."

"You know what we need to do, Thomas?"

"What?" he asked.

"We need to go and sit down with my grandma and grandad and ask them all about 1936 - and I mean everything," I said. "If we're going to try and convince people that we're from this time, we have to understand everything about the people from this year."

"Good idea."

In the shop, the man behind the counter asked, "What can I get you fine young people?" He leant down to stroke Patch and kindly filled a bowl of water for him to have a drink.

"Two lemonades for us," Iris said, and looked at me.

"Yes, two lemonades here, as well," I said.

"That's four lemonades," Iris said to the man. "And one bar of chocolate to share."

I went to put my hand in my pocket to pay, but Iris stopped me and said, "It's okay. These are on me."

Outside, Iris handed us our drinks. "Like I said, the minute you don't look like you can afford much and then go into a shop and buy four bottles of lemonade and a chocolate bar for your friends, people will start talking," she said, with a smile.

She was right, and a part of me loved the fact that even though I was the same age as my grandma and aunt Alice at the moment, they were still looking out for me.

"Here you go, Thomas, your lemonade," Iris said as she passed it over, smiling at him.

"This is the nicest lemonade I've ever tasted!" Thomas said, a little too enthusiastically.

He was right, though. We were both having a hard time with how good it was. "Me too; you can actually taste the lemons."

"Well, of course you can!" Aly scoffed. "What do you think lemonade is made out of, apples?"

All three of them started laughing at me, but I couldn't help but smile.

"Come on, then," I said, "let's keep going."

As we got to the edge of the town I could see the old bus stop that I remembered from the future, only it was new now, and a tram stop.

"Look, Thomas," I said, in an undertone. "That's still there in our time! Let's put our initials on it with your penknife and see if they're still there when we go back."

"What are you two talking about?" Aly asked, intrigued.

"We were just talking about scratching our initials in the seat," I said.

Thomas grabbed my arm. "What are you saying? They're not going to want to do that," he hissed urgently. "They'll think we're troublemakers."

But Aly said, "Good idea," which took us both by surprise.

"Who wants to do it?" Aly asked.

I nominated Thomas, as he was better at it than me.

"Thanks," he replied sourly. "Just leave it up to me to break the law, why don't you?" He laughed as he passed Patch's lead over to Iris.

"Stop complaining and start scratching," she said. "We'll sit casually around you and make sure no one can see us."

Aly looked at me and said, "This is so naughty! I'm so excited. If our mum could see us, we'd be grounded for a month."

I was beginning to get the impression that Iris and Aly's upbringing was pretty strict.

Thomas asked, "How are we going to do this?"

"Very quickly!" Iris laughed. "Why don't you write 'Thomas plus Iris' on top and then 'George plus Aly' underneath?"

"Why Thomas plus Iris?" I teased.

"Shut up, no reason," she replied and gave me a friendly push.

"Come on then, you three," Thomas said, "cover me while I do this."

"Leave room for Paul plus Em," Aly suggested.

"Good idea!" Iris said. "It'll be a nice surprise for them when they see it."

CHAPTER FOURTEEN

MESSING WITH TIME

Unbeknownst to us, 50 years in the future, David and Sean were sitting on that very bench at the old bus stop.

David was sitting on the chair with his arm around a girl and Sean was sitting on the back of the bench with his feet on the seat, showing off in front of another girl.

"Lean forward!" Sean said to David, suddenly. "How's George's name on that seat? That wasn't there before, was it?" he said.

Together, they read:

'Thomas + Iris
George + Aly
Paul + Em'

"It must've been; it's been scratched in there for years by the looks of it," David said. "It can't be our George, surely?"

"Well, all time we've been down here, I've never seen that before," Sean complained. "Just you wait until I see that George!"

"But it looks like it's been here for years!" David said.

"I know, but I can't figure out why we couldn't see it before," Sean reasoned. "So it must be something to do with our brother. And who are the girls?"

"I don't know," David said, "but it says Thomas, George and Paul, and if you read down, that's 'TGP'. Now, where have I seen those initials before?" he pondered, rubbing his chin.

Back in 1936, Thomas, Iris, Aly and I all stepped back and took a look at Thomas's handiwork.

"It looks good," Iris said. "You're quite handy with a penknife."

"Yes, but let's hope nobody saw us do it," he said, putting the knife away.

When the coast was clear we all moved away from the tram stop, glancing back at the bench.

While the girls spoke between themselves I said to Thomas, "I can't wait to have a look when we get back to see if our names are still there."

"Yes, I hope they haven't renewed the seat or that work would have been for nothing," he said.

"We'll have to sneak down town ourselves when we get back," I said.

"We'll have to be careful not to get caught by Sean or David," Thomas pointed out.

"They won't catch us," I said confidently, "and they'll never know we were there."

"We need to go to the DIY shop to get a padlock," I said to the girls.

"DIY shop?" Aly echoed. "What's one of them?"

"What does it mean?" Iris said.

"A do-it-yourself shop," I explained.

They both laughed and said that that was actually a good idea.

"Perhaps you should start one up when you've finished running away," Aly said.

"Oh no," I whispered to Thomas. "I hope we weren't the ones that came up with the abbreviation 'DIY'. We could have just broken one of the laws!"

"This is exactly why we have to try and not break them by saying the wrong thing," he said.

Ignorant of our worries, the girls led us to an iron-mongers store that was full of tools and things, including padlocks.

"This should do it," Iris said, picking up a heavy-duty lock with two keys on it. "Give me 3p and I'll go and buy it, then if the man asks, I can tell him I'm buying it for my father."

She took the 3p and the lock to the counter and started talking to the shopkeeper. Aly was looking at some 'Home Sweet Home' frames that were hanging on the wall.

I had a suspicion she was thinking about taking over the den and putting up some girly, homely things.

Iris came back with a padlock and a halfpenny in change.

"Bargain, tuppence halfpenny for a padlock," I said.

"You're joking, right?" She laughed. "That was quite expensive, but we needed a good one to make sure your money's kept safe."

"Well, time's getting on," Aly said, "we need to get home before our mum comes looking for us and we get into trouble."

So, off we went, making our way back down to the village. It was getting late and by the time we got back home it was around 6 o'clock in the evening. The dog was starving and I was beginning to feel hungry myself.

The girls walked us back to our den.

"We have about half an hour," Iris said. "Before we need to go back, can we come into your den?"

"Of course you can," Thomas said, "you don't even need to ask. In fact," he added, handing them one of the keys, "you should keep a key for the door and the gate and then if we're never here for whatever reason, you can use the place."

I nudged Thomas's arm and asked him, "Are you sure?"

"Yes," he said, without hesitation. "We can trust these girls. After all, they're your grandma and auntie," he added in an undertone, making me chuckle.

After a little while, the dog started to whine.

"What's wrong with him?" Iris asked, concerned.

"It's 6 o'clock," said Thomas. "He needs to be fed. He'll be hungry."

The truth of the matter was that Patch was used to eating at lunchtime, and we'd been out for nearly six hours more than that now. Thinking about it, I was surprised he wasn't chewing Thomas's leg off.

"Where will you get food for your dog?" Aly asked.

"We'll go in the woods and catch a rabbit," Thomas said and laughed.

"That's horrible," Iris said.

"Only joking," he assured her. "We should go back to the store and buy a tin of dog food."

"Okay then, boys," said Aly, "we're off home now. We'll see you tomorrow, yes?"

"Of course we will," I said. "Looking forward to it already."

Iris smiled as she walked out, a skip in her step, and we all left the den at the same time. Iris and Aly walked off towards the village and we walked towards the quarry.

"What a great day!" Thomas said as we walked along.

"Yes, and it's only half over," I reminded him. "When we get back it'll only be 1 o'clock. We could go for lunch, drop the dog off, and then go down town to have a look at our names on the tram bench."

"You mean the bus stop bench?"

"Oh yes! The bus stop bench," I said and laughed.

Again, as we approached the magic door, the dog started barking and pulling at his lead.

"I wonder if we can see that boy anywhere," I said.

Thomas pointed. "Look, over there by the wall. The water looks a different colour, almost like there's a grey sky above it."

"Yes, you're right," I said. "That must be how we were able to see the boy, before. We can see right through the door from over here."

"Come on, then," I said, aware we couldn't afford to become distracted so close to not one, but two, magic doors.

Thomas dragged the dog towards the door and together we went through.

"We're back," I said. "Let's go down and get changed, and then go for lunch."

"I'll leave the dog at home after lunch," Thomas said. "Should we go straight to town, or go and see your grandad to find out more about the past?"

"Down town," I said. "I'm dying to see if our names are still on the bench. I love my grandad but I don't want to spend all afternoon talking to him about the past. You know what old people are like when they get going! We'll never get out of there," I laughed.

Back home, when I walked in the house, David and Sean were sitting in the living room as if they'd been waiting for me. They both stared at me.

"What's the matter with you two?" I asked.

"You know!" David said, which told me nothing at all. "You know what."

Mum was in the kitchen, making our lunch, and Dad was in the garden, sunbathing.

"We know you've been going down town," said Sean. "And we're not quite sure how, but you scratched your name into the bus stop bench."

"No, I haven't," I said nervously. "I don't know what you're talking about. What does it say on the bench?" I asked.

"You know fine well," David said. "It says 'Thomas + Iris, George + Aly and Paul + Em'. It's a bit coincidental that your two friends are called Thomas and Paul. I don't know who the girls are, but I'm going to find out."

"How do you three know three girls?" Sean asked.

"And how did you make it look so old?" David asked. He looked genuinely curious about that.

"What are you hiding from us?" Sean demanded, cross. "Whatever it is, we're going to find out!"

Mum walked in then, interrupting. She told us that our lunches were ready. "Go and help yourselves," she said.

I grabbed my lunch and sat out in the garden with my dad. I knew my brothers wouldn't come out and hassle me about being down town with him there, or they'd drop themselves in it.

As I sat in the garden with my sandwich, my head was swimming with worries. I needed to elude Sean and David and get to Thomas before they did to let him know what they knew. I had no idea what we were going to tell Paul. So much had happened since he'd been away and he'd only been gone for one day.

"What's up with you?" Dad asked, reading the puzzlement on my face. "You look worried about something."

"Nothing," I said.

"Well, if there's anything you ever need to talk to me about, don't hesitate," he said, putting his hand on my shoulder.

"Okay, I will, Dad. I promise."

"Good," he said. "Now eat your sandwich and then go out and play. You don't want to waste this beautiful weather. You should make the most of the summer holidays - but remember, stay away from the quarry!"

"I will, Dad. I promise."

It made me feel almost sick to lie to his face, knowing that I was going down there anyway. However, I wasn't lying when I said I wasn't playing near the water, because we were going through the magic door instead.

After lunch I went out to call on Thomas. I heard Sean and David follow me out, so I ran up to Thomas's door just as he was opening it.

"Let me in," I said urgently.

"What's the matter with you?" he asked, surprised.

"It's Sean and David," I said, and pushed past him to go into the hall.

Thomas shut the door.

"They've seen our name etched into the seat up at the old tram stop and they think we've been up there, meeting girls!" I told him. "They said they're going to follow me and keep an eye on me until they find out what's going on."

"This isn't as bad as it sounds," Thomas said, after a moment's thought. "They can't tell your mum and dad about your names in the seat or they'll drop themselves in it, so that part of the problem isn't an issue," he said.

"Never mind all that!" I said. "I'm dying to go down and see our names - though it's nice to know they're there already."

"Me too," Thomas said. "We'll worry about them later."

I suggested that we go out the back door of Thomas's house to keep Sean and David from following us, then I froze as Thomas's mum came out into the hall, but she smiled.

"I know what you mean," she said, with empathy. "My older sisters used to annoy me when I was your age! Go on and sneak out the back door. I'll let the dog out and tell them you're playing in your bedroom."

"Thanks," I said, gratefully.

"Thanks, Mum," Thomas said, and off we slipped, out of the back door and across the fields.

We started walking towards the town. Things were a lot different in our time; there were a lot more buildings along the way. New houses had been built, along with new shops and roads, and even a new school.

The little shop where we'd bought lemonade with the girls was still there. It had been updated, with new windows and doors, but the rest of the building was the same.

We popped in for a look around. The only things that hadn't changed were the high ceilings and coving.

"Can I help you with anything, boys?" the shopkeeper asked.

"No, thanks. We're just looking around, thank you," I said, and then added, "actually, do you know who used to own the shop back in the 1930s?"

"Yes, why do you ask?" he asked, surprised.

"We're doing a project when we go back to school; we're learning about the past," I lied.

"Good thinking," Thomas whispered. "That's a good way of getting information out of everybody."

The shopkeeper nodded. "My father owned this shop before me, but he's retired. He's getting on now."

"Thank you," I said.

"Speak of the devil," said the shopkeeper. "Here he is, now."

And from out of the back of the shop walked a frail old man.

I nudged Thomas and said, "That's the man who served us a few hours ago!"

"I know," he said. "This is too strange."

We left the shop and headed up to the town, heading straight for our bench. Sure enough, our names were still there, deeply scored into the wooden seat:

"Look at that," I said. "It looks like it's been there for 50 years, yet we only put it there this morning."

We both smiled.

"It's like the tree, actually," I said. "Look at the initials! It says 'TGP', the same as we etched into the tree down by the rope swing."

"Oy! You two!" we heard Sean shouting, and my heart sank. "Come here."

We didn't move, so they ran up to us.

"What are you doing here?" David asked.

"I wanted to see the names in the bench you were on about," I told him, which was mostly true.

"If Dad finds out you're down town, he'll kill you," Sean reminded me.

"If Dad finds out you're here, he'll kill you, too!" I said, confident.

"Just be careful and remember who you're talking to," Sean said, getting in my face. "I'm your older brother!"

"There," David said, pointing. "You, Thomas and Paul have your name etched in that bench. So, explain?"

Thomas said, "Look at it, you idiot. It's over 50 years old by the looks of it - it's been there for years. How could we have done that?"

"I don't know," Sean said, "but I'm going to find out. And when I find the girls I'm going to tell them to stay away from you and that you're losers!"

Me and Thomas walked away, rolling our eyes.

"Don't worry about what they said," Thomas advised. "They're the losers. Isn't it funny that they don't know it's their grandma, auntie Alice, and auntie Em?"

"I know!" I laughed. "It's really funny. There is something we need to do, though," I went on. "We need to hide the clothes that we get changed into in the den. We can't risk Sean or David seeing us getting changed or walking around in the old clothes. They're going to be on us like a rash from now on."

Thomas agreed, and we decided we'd keep everything in the den, including the watches.

We made our way back down towards the village. When we got there, we noticed Paul's mum's car was back.

"Great," I said, "we need to go and see if he's coming out. We've got a lot to tell him!"

We agreed it would be a good idea to tell my grandma and grandad that we were doing a school project, like the shopkeeper, and take pens and notepads to pretend to be putting our homework together.

As we walked up Paul's path, he came to the door.

"Are you coming out?" I asked.

"Yes, I've got a few hours, my mum said."

"Good! We have so much to tell you - you're not going to believe the day we've had," said Thomas.

"Did you find out where my grandma lived?" he asked, excited.

"Yes, she lives in Ash Meadows," Thomas replied. "We've been to her house."

"What do you mean, Thomas?" he asked, surprised. "Have you been in?"

"No, we went to the shop and asked the shopkeeper where she lived," he explained. "She told us she lived down by the old church. When we went down there we hid behind the wall and we heard her mum - your great grandma - shout for Elsa."

"Did she see you?"

"Not at first," I said. "But when we rode past her on our bikes she did look and smile."

"Your bikes? Did you take them through the magic door?" he asked, wide-eyed.

We told him the story of how we got the bikes with the money Grandad gave us.

"Come on, let's go down the rope swing and we'll fill you in on everything," I said. "But later we need to go and see my grandma and grandad."

"Why?" he asked.

"We've come up with a plan to find out all about 1936," I explained, and told him our idea.

"That's a good idea," Paul said.

At the swing, we told Paul all the things we'd done since he'd been at his aunt and uncle's house. We told him about the bikes and the den, the story we'd told the girls, giving them a key to the den, and riding on the tram.

"We think we've found another magic door," Thomas told him, "but it's over the water and we can't get to it. We put it on the map, though."

"Tell him about the thing with the rock," I said, so Thomas did.

"Maybe it just didn't make a splash because it landed in the grass?" he suggested.

"Yes," I said, "I could have believed that myself if the rock hadn't come flying back a few moments later!" I laughed.

"You're joking!" he said. "Someone actually threw it back?"

"I know," I said. "Somebody over there is very unhappy with us!"

We all laughed.

We also told him that we went down town to the old tram stop (now the bus stop) and etched our names into the seat.

"You went down town?" he gasped.

"Yes," I said. "We figured if we're already travelling back in time, going down town is a walk in the park!"

"What about Sean and David?"

"About them... we think they're onto us," I said. "They're definitely trying to follow us. They saw our names carved into the seat at the bus stop and they know something's going on, but they can't quite put their finger on it."

We decided to take Paul into town so he could see his name carved into the bench.

"Tell me about the den," he said, on the way.

"Yes, the den!" I said. "A boy's den that Thomas gave a girl the key to!"

"So?" Thomas said. "I gave a key to a girl, but remember those girls are your grandma and auntie Alice, so they're not just any old girls! And, technically, Iris paid for it with the money her and your grandad gave you," he said, and laughed.

Paul said, "I've only been away for a few days and you've already had an adventure of a lifetime! I'm really not looking forward to going on holiday anymore. I want to stay here with you."

"When do you go?" I asked.

"We've put it off, now," he told us. "It's Grandma's funeral in two days, then we go off two days after that."

We worked out that we had at least three days where we could go backwards and forwards, since Paul was likely to be busy on the day of the funeral.

"We could get you a bike on the other side and the three of us could ride to Ash Meadows so you could see where your grandma lived," I said.

"I think it's probably better if we walk," Thomas remarked, amused. "Those bikes are rough."

A short while later, we arrived at the town's old bus stop. The bus had just left, so there was no one on the seat.

"Not bad," said Paul approvingly, looking at the names on the bench. "Not bad at all!"

It was getting late, given that we'd walked into town, and we needed to get back home in time for tea.

"Let's go," I said. "We can plan tomorrow's trip, all three of us."

And so we did. On the way home, we talked and laughed and joked about what we were going do the next day, and soon we were about to pass where the old allotments were.

"Come on, Paul," said Thomas. "We'll show you where our new den is."

As we walked up the path alongside the allotments, we noticed our allotment was one of the worst ones there, with badly erected fencing, an old, dilapidated greenhouse with no windows, and some old, smashed up concrete slabs where the den once sat.

"What do you think?" Thomas asked.

Paul laughed and said, "Well, I hope it looks better than this tomorrow."

"I've got an idea!" I said. "Why don't we bury something in the allotment back in time and then come back and dig it up?"

"That sounds like a good idea!" Thomas said. "What should we bury? Should we get something from this time and take it back and bury it, or take something from their time?"

"Well," I said, thinking, "if we take something from this time, take it back and bury it, then get it back, it will just be something old from this day and age. However, if we get something from the other side and bury it, when we come back it'll be an antique."

"Good point," said Paul.

"We could ask to borrow something from one of the girls," I said.

"We can't borrow it," Thomas said, with a grin. "We wouldn't be giving it back for at least 50 years."

"Okay then, why don't we ask the girls if we can borrow something, pretend to lose it, bury it, and then when we come back, dig it up and go and give it back to whoever lent it to us, telling them we found it here," I said.

"That seems a little bit cruel. Doesn't it break one of the laws?" Thomas asked.

"Well, it is a little cruel," I agreed, "but we won't take anything that we think is valuable, so we're only bending the laws instead of breaking them, so what harm could it do?"

"When are we going to your grandad's to learn about the olden days?" Thomas asked.

"We can go after tea, if you like?" I suggested.

So, after tea, we all met up as agreed in the village. "Let's go and call on Grandma and Grandad and ask if they can tell us a little bit about the past," I said.

With our notepads in hand, we went to call at their house. I knocked on the door and Grandad answered.

"What can I do for you three scallywags?" he laughed.

"Hi, Grandad!" I said brightly. "We just wanted to know if you wouldn't mind answering a few questions about the past?"

"The past?" he asked.

"Yes, we have a school project to hand in at the start of the autumn term and we need to learn about the past," I said.

"Okay, come on in," he said. "Sit down there and I'll ask your Grandma to get us all a drink. What would you all like, Coke?"

"Yes," we all said at the same time.

Grandad left the room, so I stood up and started looking at the photos on the wall.

"Look at this photo," I said. "It's of the store opening in town, the new Co-op. It's the one that has the brown paper over the windows."

"What store are you talking about?" Paul asked.

"There's a new Co-op store opening up in town in the next couple of days - back in the past," I said. "This must be a photo done on the day it opened."

"Do you recognise anybody in it?" Thomas asked, as we all stood up to look at the photo.

"I recognise that man there!" I said, pointing him out. "I think that was Grandma's and Auntie Alice's uncle, who worked at the butchers."

"I think you're right," Thomas said.

"Look," Paul said, "that looks like your grandma, auntie Alice, and auntie Em at the end."

He was right! It *was* them. I was so excited.

Just then, Grandma walked through the door with a tray of drinks.

"When was this taken?" I asked her.

"Well, now. Let's see - summer, 1936," she said. "I remember it well," she added, with a smile. "It was a really hot summer and the holidays seemed to last forever."

Grandad came back in. "Come on, then," he said. "What do you want to ask?"

"We just wanted to ask about the old school, the town, the shops, and what kind of things you used to get up to when you were our age?" I said.

"Well," Grandma said, with a laugh. "If we tell you what we used to get up to, you mustn't tell your mum or dad because we used to tell them off for doing those things."

"A little hypocritical, I know," said Grandad. "But that was our job as parents."

"What kind of things did you get up to?" I asked.

"Me, Alice, and Em used to play down in the old quarry," she told us, as Grandad nodded. "Only it wasn't as old in those days! We would make rope swings and climb trees and play with boys, but we shouldn't have. It was naughty!" She chuckled.

"Why was playing with boys naughty?" I asked, interested.

She shrugged. "No real reason. It was just an old-fashioned thing. Girls would play with girls and boys would play with boys."

"We didn't have any of the toys you three have today," Grandad said. "You kids don't know you're born."

Grandma told us about some of the playground games the girls used to play, and all about the shops in the town. Grandma did most of the talking while Grandad nodded along in agreement. He didn't seem to want to tell us much, he was just happy to let Grandma fill us in and occasionally he'd add a detail of his own.

"What about Auntie Alice and Auntie Em?" I asked.

"Yes," said Paul, "we noticed you're in the photo on the wall with them."

"He means George pointed them out to us," said Thomas, delivering a swift kick to him under the table to remind him he shouldn't know what they looked like at that age.

"Yes," she said. "We used to hang about together almost all of the time. We weren't only sisters, but best friends."

"Did you ever hang out with anybody else?" I asked. "What about the boys?"

Thomas nudged my leg, as if to say, 'You're asking too many questions'.

"Yes," Grandma said. "We did meet some boys in the summer holidays. Boys from another village."

I was about to ask more about them, but Grandad leaned forward. "Come on, then, boys, let's be having you. Grandma and I haven't had our tea yet."

"Okay then, Grandad. Thanks for telling us about the past," I said.

"No problem, mate," he said as he shook my hand and then pulled me in for a hug.

Outside, Thomas said. "That was cut short a little bit, wasn't it? Just as well, really. We can't ask too many questions about the boys they met. We don't want to arouse any suspicion."

"You're paranoid," Paul said. "Not in a million years are they going to think that we're the same boys they met 50 years ago."

The next morning, after breakfast and chatting with my mum, I went outside where I found Thomas and Paul waiting for me.

"Everybody ready?" I asked, and off we went to the rope swing to get the clothes from the vault.

"What should we do today?" I asked.

"I thought we were going to get something from one of the girls and bury it in the allotment?" Thomas said.

We got ready and made our way towards the magic door.

"So, the plan is, we go through the magic door and go straight to Ash Meadows, to Paul's grandma's house?"

"No," Paul said. "I want to see the den, first."

"Okay, we can go there first," I said. "We'll need some money to take if we're going to Ash Meadows."

We walked up to the magic door, crouched down, and went through. On the other side, the coast was clear.

"Let's go to the den, then," I said.

As we started walking towards the allotment, Paul said, "It does look strange - seeing it now, when only a few hours ago it was a wreck."

"I know, it's hard to get your head around, isn't it?" I agreed. "But isn't it exciting?"

We unlocked the gate and walked down towards the den.

"Look, Thomas," I said. "The padlock's not on the door!"

We all stopped in our tracks.

"Somebody must be in there," I said.

"But who?" Paul asked.

Slowly and carefully, we edged our way towards the den, where we could hear a girl's laughter. We all let out a sigh of relief.

"It's the girls!" I said. "They're in there. They must have let themselves in with the key Thomas gave them."

We went down and opened the door and sure enough, the three girls were sitting inside, two on the stools and one on the floor.

"Hello!" Aly said.

"What have you done with our den?" I asked, shocked.

On the walls were pictures of flowers and 'Home Sweet Home' frames. There were hand-knitted cushions on our tree stump stools, and everything was much cleaner.

"We made it homely," Aly said proudly.

I looked at Thomas and said, "Well, this is what happens when you give a girl a key."

"Leave Thomas alone," said Iris. "We've made the place look nice; you should be thanking us."

"Okay, thank you, girls, for turning our man-pad into a girl-pad," Paul said, and we all laughed.

"This must be what my dad keeps going on about, when he says women take over and try and change everything," I complained.

"That's right," Aly said cheerfully, "women rule the world, so get used to it!"

The girls laughed.

"What are you boys up to today?" Aly asked.

We're off to Ash Meadows to see Paul's cousin," Thomas said. "You can come with us, if you want."

I turned and looked at him and tried to ask what he was thinking without saying anything out loud. What were we going to say when we get there and Paul's cousin wasn't there?

Luckily, Aly said, "No, we can't go that far. We'll get into trouble if we get found out and then we'll be grounded for the rest of the summer."

That was a close one, I thought. "Well, we're off now," we said.

"Okay," Iris said. "We'll stay here, if that's okay?"

"Of course it is," Thomas said. "What's ours is yours."

They smiled at each other.

As we set off I whispered to Thomas, "You're going to have to stop inviting Iris everywhere. You could have dropped us right in it - imagine getting into Ash Meadows and the girls asking where Paul's cousin lives!"

"I just forget, that's all."

"That's because you fancy my grandma," I said, cross.

"Don't say it like that," he said. "It sounds wrong when you say it like that. Your grandma's an old lady."

We all laughed.

"Yes, she's an old lady. She's my grandma, and you're my friend. It's important that you don't ever get too close to her," I warned him.

"That's alright," Paul said, grinning, "just keep reminding him that she's your grandma and an old lady."

"That's what I'll do," I said. "I'll get a photo of my grandma and keep it in my back pocket, and every time he looks at her I'll show him the photo."

Paul and I laughed out loud.

"Okay, you two. I get it," said Thomas grumpily. "She's an old lady."

After an hour or so, we approached the village of Ash Meadows. We got to the shop first.

"Let's go in and get some lemonade and some food," I said.

"Okay," said Thomas.

"Yeah," said Paul, "I'm starving."

"Is this the shop where the lady told you where my grandma lived?" Paul asked.

"Yes, the lady knows your grandma's family," I said, as we walked through the door.

"Hello again, boys. Back for some more lemonade?" the shopkeeper asked. She must have remembered us from the other day. "I see you brought a friend with you?"

As we walked through, looking on the shelves for the lemonade and some food, I noticed Paul had stopped and was looking at someone out of my line of sight.

"Paul," I said, "what are you looking at?"

"That girl over there," he said, shocked, "that's my grandma. I can just tell."

I looked over. "He's right, Thomas," I said. "Quick, over here, you can't be seen."

We hid behind the shelves.

"How did you know that was your grandma?" I asked.

"I don't know; I just had this feeling that I knew her."

"Well, technically you do," Thomas pointed out. "She's your grandma. Maybe you saw photos of her from that age?"

Elsa hadn't seen us, so we stayed hidden while she was served by the lady and left.

"We're going to have to make sure we don't bump into her," I said.

"Why?" Paul asked. "You talk to your grandma, what's the difference?"

"He's right," Thomas said, "what difference would it make?"

I didn't really know. I just had a feeling that it wasn't a good idea. "I don't suppose it could do any harm if we went and said hello, could it?"

We grabbed our bottles of lemonade and some pork pies, then paid the shopkeeper on the way out. "Come on, then, you two. Let's go down to Paul's grandma's house and see if we can try and make friends."

On the way to Elsa's house we noticed her still walking towards home.

"There she is," Paul said, sounding astonished, "there's my grandma."

"Remember, Paul," I said, "she's called Elsa, here, not Grandma."

"I know. It's a bit strange, though."

Just then, she turned around and looked right at all three of us.

"Hello," she said.

"Hello," we all replied.

She stopped walking and we carried on up to her. It was as if the cat had got all of our tongues. We didn't know what else to say. With the exception of Aly, Iris and Em, we were all rather shy around girls.

After a short, awkward silence she laughed. "Are you three alright?"

"Yes," I said, "we're just not used to girls talking to us."

"Well, let me help," she said. "My name's Elsa and I live down the road. What about you?"

I started to relax and told her, "My name's George, and this is Thomas and Paul."

"Hello, Thomas, Paul, and George," she said.

"Where are you from?" she asked. "You don't live in Ash Meadows."

"We're from Meadow View," said Thomas.

"We've been playing in the village, but we were starting to get bored, so we've decided to venture out," I said.

"I'm guessing your parents don't know you're this far out," she remarked.

"No," Thomas said. "You know what parents are like, we'd be grounded for the rest of the school holidays."

She laughed. "Yes, I know! It would be the same for me, my mum is so strict. If I even get caught talking to boys I'll be grounded, and she keeps threatening to send me off to boarding school."

That's not nice, I thought to myself.

"So, George. That's a nice name," she said and smiled at me.

"Thank you," I replied.

Paul coughed, perhaps as a reminder not to change anything, and Elsa and I took unconscious steps away from one another. With a jolt, I realised that I liked her - and from the way she was smiling at me, she might like me, too.

"I have to go and take this bread home, but I can come out and play afterwards, if you'd like?" she said.

"Yes," Paul and me both said at exactly the same time.

She laughed. "Wait here and I'll be back."

Paul said, "I'm so excited that I'm going to get to know my grandma, after all these years of knowing her."

"While we're on the subject of grandmas, George," Thomas said, "what was that?"

"What was what?" I asked nonchalantly, though I knew what he meant.

"Shut up," I said after a moment. "I've only just met her and I wasn't looking at her like anything!"

"Stop it, you two," Paul said, pulling a face. "That's my grandma you're talking about and it's weird."

Thomas threatened to do the same thing as I'd suggested and bring a photo of Paul's grandma as an old lady to keep reminding me. I shuddered and thought, *he's right.*

We couldn't talk much more about it, to my relief, because Elsa was now coming back up the road towards us.

"Hi, boys," she said brightly, "what do you want to do, then?"

"I don't know," I said. "What is there around here to do?"

"Not a lot," she replied. "There's a forest down there," she pointed to it, "and a little stream running through it, but apart from that, not a lot. What about where you live?"

"Just the same," I said. "Not a lot to do, not a lot happening."

There was a play area at the other end of the village, we'd noticed on our way over, so I suggested we went there. When we got to the park there was an old wooden climbing frame, two swings, and a seesaw.

Elsa went and sat on the swing. I wanted to join her, but I knew Paul wanted to talk and get to know her, so I said, "I'll be over in a little while, Thomas and me are going to play on the seesaw."

"Okay," she said, as Paul jumped onto the swing next to her.

While Thomas and I played on the seesaw, we watched Paul talking to his grandma.

"I wonder what they're talking about," Thomas reflected.

"I don't know, but I hope he doesn't slip up and say anything he shouldn't! We don't want to break any more laws."

We stayed there for a few hours, talking and laughing, and getting along really well. Eventually, of course, we had to go.

"We have to go now, Elsa," I said.

"So soon?" she replied, crestfallen. "I was having fun."

"Maybe you can come to our village one day," I said.

"I'd love to," she said, "but I have to be careful that my mum doesn't find out, or like I said, I'd be grounded forever!" She frowned at the thought, but then smiled again. "Just in case I manage to sneak out, how do I get there and how will I know how to find you?"

Before I had a chance to answer, Paul jumped in. "Don't worry, we'll come and get you and we can go back there together."

"Great," she replied, pleased. "Goodbye, then," she said as she walked off towards home.

We all shouted goodbye at the same time.

As we started walking home, Thomas asked Paul, "Well then, what was it like to meet your grandma?"

"It was amazing," he said, bouncing up and down on the balls of his feet as he walked. "She's a wonderful person! I can't believe that I never got to know her as my grandma."

He started to well up, his eyes shedding a tear that rolled down his face. "I can't believe she's gone," he said, with a hoarse voice.

"Yes, but cheer up," I said. "How many people can go back and meet their family after they've died? You're very lucky."

"He's right," Thomas agreed, "you should just make the most of knowing her, here and now."

We carried on, walking back to our village in silence.

As we got to the den we noticed that the man who looked after the allotments was there at our gate, talking to the man we kept seeing around the place - the same man who'd stopped me walking in front of the tram and who distracted the policeman by the school.

We waited for a little while, out of sight, and after a short time we saw him shake the allotment keeper's hand before walking off. Just then the allotment keeper spotted us.

"Hello, boys," he said. "You just missed your uncle.

He'd signed for the allotment, so it's yours now to look after for the next 12 months. I'll collect the next three months' payments about 11 weeks from now, so have fun!"

We looked at each other in complete and utter shock.

"What does he mean, my uncle? Nobody knows we're here!" I said, flabbergasted.

Paul and Thomas both looked at me. "What's going on here?" Thomas asked. "How can he be your uncle? And how does he know that the allotment needed signing for?"

"I'm scared," Paul admitted. "I'm frightened. It's like someone's watching us and knows what's going on. I want to go home."

"Me too!" Thomas said.

"We need to find out who he is, how he knows us, and if he knows we're time travelling," I said.

I spotted the girls as they walked up to the allotment gate. "We need to get rid of them!" I said. "At least while we try and find out what just happened."

"We have to go now, boys," Aly said. "It's getting late and we have to go."

I thought, *that's good timing!*

"We'll see you tomorrow?" I asked aloud.

"No," she said. "You won't see us for about four days; we're off to see our auntie down country, and we won't be back for a few days. Don't forget, when we get back the town fair is just a few days later for the new Co-op shop opening."

"We'll come with you," Thomas offered.

"You can't," Aly replied. "Our parents are taking us up, but you can still come and we can meet you there. We'll tell our parents we're going off to play."

I kept nudging Thomas's arm to tell him to let the girls go because we needed to talk about what had just happened.

"Okay then, girls," Thomas said. "We'll see you when you get back."

Just before the girls left, something caught my eye and I said to Aly, "What's this on the wall?"

"It's a medal that belongs to my grandad," she said. "I've put it there to make the place look nice."

I thought it looked good hanging there.

"But won't your grandad notice it's missing?"

"No," she said. "It just sits in the drawer upstairs. He never looks at it or gets it out. But it's a war medal, so look after it."

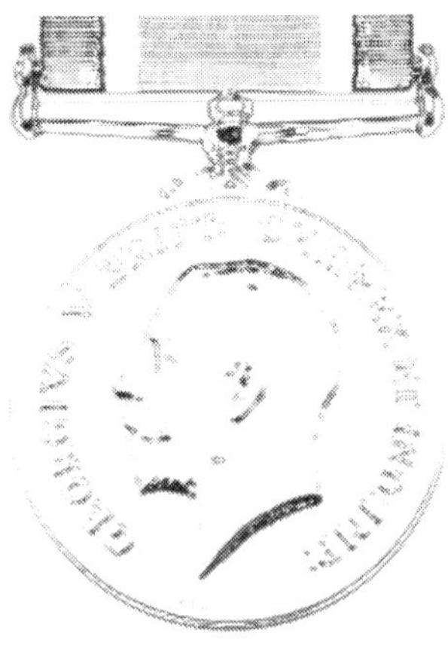

Off they went then, saying goodbye as they walked off, leaving us behind in the den.

"What are we going to do about this man we keep seeing?" I said, as soon as they were gone. "And who do you think he is?"

"I don't know," Thomas said. "Maybe he's another time traveller, like us, but if he is then why's he signing for our allotment?"

"Whoever he is, he seems to be on our side," said Paul. "He pulled you out of the way of that tram, and he's given his signature, too."

"We just need to keep an eye out for him," I said, to mutual agreement.

It was time for us to go home, but as we got ready to leave, Thomas suggested, "We could bury the medal and then get back to dig it up."

"You heard what Aly said," Paul replied. "It means a lot to her and we agreed we'd only bury something that didn't mean anything."

"Yes," I said, "but could you imagine how excited she'd be when I give it back in 50 years and tell her we found it at this allotment?"

"Where should we bury it?" Thomas asked.

I said, "First of all, we need to protect it."

We looked around and Thomas spotted an empty jar on the shelf.

"This should protect it for 50 years," I said, screwing the lid back on.

We decided to bury it where no one would find it, so we lifted a couple of the concrete slabs that made up the greenhouse floor. We'd seen the greenhouse in our time, so we knew it would still be there.

We pulled the middle slab up and dug down about a foot.

"It will be safe here," I said. "See you again in 50 years," I said to the medal as I pushed it into the hole.

I covered it over and Thomas put the slab back down. Then, with the slab down, we all jumped up and down on top of it to flatten and level it back out again.

"Let's go home and see if it's still there," I said.

Chapter Fifteen

The Harsh Reality

After changing our clothes at the den and leaving them there so Sean and David wouldn't find them, we walked to the magic door and went straight to the allotments.

"There!" I said. "Look at the greenhouse from 10 minutes ago, all dilapidated and falling apart."

One of the gardeners looked up at us and we made ourselves scarce. We couldn't dig up our treasure right away as people might see us, and we didn't own it in this time.

"I think we should come out after tea," I said, as we hurried away. "Maybe about 7 o'clock? There shouldn't be anyone around by then."

"Okay," Paul agreed.

"What time is it now?" Thomas asked.

I looked at my watch. "It's only 2 o'clock. Let's go home for lunch."

As we got into the village we saw Grandad.

"Hello, George," he said. "Your mum and dad have had to go out and get some more paint for your bedroom and they've asked if you want to have your lunch around ours?"

I loved going to Grandma and Grandad's for lunch, so I jumped at the chance.

"We're off then," Thomas said.

Paul said, "See you after lunch."

"Okay, see you soon," I said.

I went with Grandad and when we went in I could smell home-made chips! My Grandma made the best chips in the whole world. She would cut them thinly and then drop them into red hot lard, cooking them for just the right amount of time and serving them up with two runny fried eggs and fresh cut bread - as thick as my arm - with lashings of real butter on top.

This was one my favourite meals and only Grandma could get it exactly right.

"Sit down at the table," she said. "Your dinner will be here in a minute."

"I'll give you a hand, Iris," Grandad said.

Alone in the room, I went to look at all the old photos hanging on the walls. The one of the Co-Op opening that I'd looked at the day before caught my eye. Something was different; I frowned. Auntie Alice was missing from the photo. Her two sisters were there, but Aly was nowhere to be seen. I went cold all over, just as my grandma walked in with my lunch.

"What's the matter with you?" she asked.

"Where's Alice?" I asked, worried. "Is she okay?"

"Yes, of course she's okay," said Grandma. "I think she's at home, why?"

"No reason," I said hurriedly. "I've just noticed she's not in the photo and I thought I saw her in it yesterday."

"No," Grandma said. "Alice wasn't allowed to go down town that day because she'd been grounded."

"Grounded?"

"Yes. My dad - your grandad - grounded her for the whole of the summer holidays," Grandma explained.

I swallowed. What could have happened that meant Aly was grounded? It had to be something to do with us, but what could we have done?

I started to eat my lunch, rushing it down.

Grandad said, "You'll end up choking. What's the hurry?"

"Nothing!" I said. "I just want to go back and play."

But really, I needed to go and see Thomas and Paul and tell them about Aly. We had to figure out what had gone wrong.

I almost inhaled my food, burning my mouth on the hot chips. There was egg all over my face and I guzzled down the cola drink Grandma had given me.

For the first time in my life I didn't enjoy the meal.

"I have to go, now, Grandma, Grandad," I said. "I'm sorry to have to eat and run."

"That's okay, mate," Grandad said. "You run along and do what you have to do."

"Bye, then," I shouted as I ran out of the door, "I'll see you tomorrow!"

When I got to Thomas's house, I ran up to the door and started knocking as hard as I could. His mum came to the door.

"What's wrong with you?" she asked, worried. "What's the emergency?"

"Nothing," I said. "I just wanted to see if Thomas was coming out!"

I think he knew something was up, because I saw him wolf down the rest of his lunch behind his mum.

"What the matter with you?" he said, when we were outside. "What's the panic? You look like you've seen a ghost!"

"Something's going on, something's gone wrong!" I said, on the edge of panic. "We need to find out what it is, then put it right!"

"Calm down," he said, "you're getting too excited and not making any sense."

I told him that we needed to go and get Paul, and then go to visit my auntie Alice.

"Why your auntie Alice?"

"Let's go and get Paul and I'll tell you all about it."

When we got there, he was just coming out the door.

"What's the matter, George?" he asked, when he caught sight of my face. "Why are you all pale and upset?"

"I need to tell you something," I said. "I've just been around Grandad's house and looked at the picture on the wall of everyone standing outside the Co-Op."

"Yes?" Thomas asked.

"Auntie Alice wasn't in the photo!"

"She was," Paul insisted. "I saw it myself, just yesterday."

Thomas agreed.

"I know," I said. "I saw it, too, but today she's missing!"

They both stared at me in shock.

Horrified, Paul asked, "Is your auntie Alice still alive?"

"Yes, but when I asked Grandma about the photo and why Auntie Alice wasn't in it, she said it was because she was grounded for the entire summer holidays that year and wasn't allowed to go with them that day."

Thomas replied, "Well, she was in the photo yesterday, but not today, so what have we done in the past that could have changed things?"

"It has to be the medal!" Paul realised. "That's the only thing we've done."

"I don't know," I said. "I think the only thing we can do is go and see Auntie Alice and ask her what happened. Then we can go back and put it right."

"But how are we going to ask her why she was grounded in 1936?" Paul asked. "It's a weird thing to want to know."

Thomas frowned and said, "We should go to the allotment, dig up the medal and then go around and tell her we found it and see if she recognises it. That way, we might find out what went wrong."

"I'm sure she'll be happy when she sees it," I said, cheering up, "but we can't let her know we know it's hers."

"Okay," said Paul.

"I bet she'll be over the moon!" Thomas said.

We wasted no time, going straight to the allotment to retrieve the medal. Being careful no one would see us, we crept around the back of the plot where our 1936 den was. Everything was quiet. The fence was in poor condition; all that remained were four strands of barbed wire stretched between wooden posts.

Thomas and I climbed through the barbed wire fence and ran in a crouch towards the old greenhouse, while Paul waited and kept an eye out for anyone coming.

"This is the slab we buried it under, it's still here!" Thomas said, excited.

"Good, let's lift it up, grab the jar, and get out of here," I said.

He lifted the slab backwards on itself and I started digging at the hole with an old stick, where I thought the jar was. After a minute or two, my stick hit something that wasn't soil.

"I can feel it!" I said.

I started digging faster. At first, all that came out of the hole were small shards of broken glass.

"We must have broken the jar when we put the slab back!" I realised. "I hope the medal's okay."

Thomas reached in. "I've got it," he said, carefully extracting the tattered ribbon out of the hole.

"That's it!" I said, as we both peered at it. "But look at the state of it, the ribbon is almost completely rotten and the medal looks black."

"I still think your auntie Alice will be pleased to see it," Thomas said. "And in this state you can see that it's been buried for years."

"I suppose you're right," I said, lowering the slab back down. "Let's get out of here and go and at least try to clean it up."

Paul waved us over, "Come on, you two," he hissed urgently. "I think someone's coming!"

We quickly climbed back through the barbed wire fence and ran up towards the village.

We cleaned our hands up as best we could in the stream, then brushed the worst of the dirt off the medal.

"Okay," I said, "let's go and see Aly."

"I bet she'll be chuffed to bits!" Thomas said.

"I hope so," I replied, as we walked towards her house.

I was imagining the look of surprise on her face and how happy she would be.

When we got there, we knocked on the door with a mixture of excitement and nerves. We didn't know how she was going to react, but it was certainly going to be interesting.

Auntie Alice came to the door with a big smile on her face. For a moment, I could see young Aly in her expression, and not just the elderly lady I knew. It was weird, but I was glad to see her after the scare with the photograph.

"Good afternoon, boys, what brings you round here?" she asked.

"Hi Auntie Alice!" I said. "We wanted to come around and see you, and ask you some questions about the past for our school project."

"I suppose you'd better come in, then," she said, with a smile. "Take off your shoes and come through. Would you like a drink?"

We gave her a chorus of "Yes, please!"

Digging was thirsty work.

She ushered us into the living room and went into the kitchen, where we could hear her moving glasses around.

"How we can do this?" I whispered.

"I don't know," said Thomas, "Just tell her that we were playing down the allotments and found it. Ask if she could tell us if it was from the olden days. She'll be chuffed to bits!"

She came in with four glasses of squash and put them down on the table.

Sitting down, she asked, "What can I tell you about the past?"

"Just things like what you got up to and who you played with," I said. I dug in my pocket for the medal and held it out. "Also, we found this old medal down by the allotments and wanted to know if you thought it was old?"

She leant forward in her chair. "Go on," she said, "show me!" Gently, she took the medal from me and examined it, before pressing her fingers to her mouth in shock. A tear started rolling down her cheek. "Where did you find this?" she asked softly.

"We found it in the allotments," I said, feeling uncertain.

She seemed very upset and confused, which wasn't what we'd been expecting.

"Do you recognise it?" Thomas asked, in a hushed voice.

"Yes," she said. "It was stolen from me by some friends… or at least, I thought they were friends. We were close friends and I thought I could trust them, but they said they'd lost the medal. At the time I thought they'd stolen it, but if you found it there, maybe they did lose it after all. It belonged to my dad and when he noticed it was missing, he went absolutely berserk. He grounded me for the entire school summer holidays, and he never trusted me with anything again after that."

She sat back in the chair, crying and wiping her eyes. "Could you please leave me alone now? I need to be on my own."

We all got up and quietly made our way towards the door.

"I'm sorry, boys," she said as we went, "but I'm so upset right now. This caused a lot of trouble in our family and I'm going to try to find out what happened to it. I'll see you in a few days, George, and I'm sure everything will be okay. Thank you again for bringing it to me," she said, and kissed me on the head before closing the door.

"I can't believe it!" I said to my friends, when we got outside. "I can't believe this was all our fault. I felt so bad in there!" I started to cry.

We had ruined her life and it was all our fault. We had felt so justified, doing that pointless experiment. We should never have taken the medal, or buried it.

"It was a stupid idea, yes. So what are we going to do about it?" Thomas asked, looking like he felt just as bad as I did.

"We have to go back and dig it up, and put it back on the wall as if nothing has happened," Paul said.

"He's right," Thomas added. "They're away for a few days, so if we do it soon she'll never notice it's gone missing. When they get back we'll have to encourage her to take it back home before her dad sees it's gone!"

"We can't go until later on tonight or we'll see our other selves," I reminded them. "We must be extra careful not to get caught.

"Come on, then," Paul said. "Let's get down the woods and wait it out for a few hours."

We had come to an important realisation: anything we did in the past had major repercussions. It only took the smallest thing to change someone's life forever.

Hours later, back at the allotments in 1936, we pulled up the pavement slabs. Thomas held the slab up, while I dug out the broken jar.

"Got it," I said, at last. "Let's go to the den and put it back."

"Job done," Paul said, as I hung it back on the wall. "Now, let's go back and see if it worked."

"I'll go back to Grandad's first, to see if I can see her in the picture," I suggested.

After having passed back through the door, we were walking up to the village when something occurred to me.

I said, "We should go and see if the pavement slabs have been moved, or if there'd ever been anything there in the last 50 years."

"Well it would have," Paul said, confused. "It was there earlier this afternoon, wasn't it?"

"Yes, but if you think about it, we've changed time," I told him. "It still shouldn't have moved."

"Are you sure?" Paul asked.

"Not completely," I said. "Let's go down and have a look!"

When we got to the allotments the barbed wire fence was just the same and it looked like nobody had been there for a while.

"Look, the grass is still long where we walked through and the barbed wire hasn't been bent out of shape where we climbed through, earlier," I said.

For a moment, all three of us stared at the fence. It was a peculiar feeling, knowing that we'd been there, but seeing that our actions in the past had erased things in our own lifetimes.

"Come on, let's go in and lift the slab," Thomas said.

It was obvious that the slab hadn't been moved in years.

"It looks like it hasn't been lifted up," Thomas observed.

"I know," I replied. "Let's lift it up to see if there's a hole underneath, or any glass. Paul, keep a lookout."

He nodded and moved back over to the fence as Thomas started lifting the slab.

"It's heavy. Can you see anything?" he asked.

"Yes, and there's no hole," I said. "It doesn't look like anything was ever there."

Thomas dropped the slab, looked at me and said, "We need to sit down and think about this. All three of us remember moving this slab earlier today."

"Yes," I said, as we left the allotments, "but today, when we went back this evening, the pavement slabs hadn't been moved because we never lifted it up this afternoon! If you think about it, the medal wasn't left in the hole in 1936 because we went back to put it back in the den. Which means we couldn't have dug it up this afternoon, because it wasn't there for us to find."

"So, what you're saying is that we've changed the past in both 1936 and 1986, even though for us they were both just today?" Paul said.

"I think so."

"My head hurts," Thomas remarked.

"Mine, too," Paul replied. He shook his head and rolled his eyes.

"We should go to your grandad's and see if your auntie Alice is back in the old photo," Thomas said.

It was nearly dinnertime, so I told Thomas and Paul that I needed to ask my mum if I could have my dinner around Grandad's - that way I could just casually look at the photo without them getting suspicious, or asking questions.

"If she says yes, I'll see you outside my grandad's house in one hour," I said. "And if she's back in the photo we can go to see Auntie Alice and make sure everything's okay there, too."

So, Paul and Thomas went home and I ran to my house and asked my mum if I could have dinner at my grandma and grandad's house.

"Yes," she replied, "as long as it's okay with them."

Grandma and Grandad were pleased to see me.

"Hello, trouble! What brings you around here, twice in one day?" Grandma asked, giving me a hug.

"Come on in, then, mate," Grandad said.

"Hi Grandma, I was just wondering if you would make me egg and chips again for my dinner?" I asked. "I had to rush it earlier and it's my favourite."

"Okay," she said. "No problem, we were just about to have ours, so you can eat with us. This time try to eat it without inhaling it," she said and laughed. "Come on, you," she said, to Grandad. "Give me a hand with the potatoes."

As soon as they'd left the room I hurried over to the photo on the wall to see if I could see Alice. I couldn't believe my eyes! To my relief, there she was, right back where she belonged.

We did it! We put time back the way it should be, I thought to myself.

Grandad walked in and found me peering at the picture. "Looking at that photo again, I see?"

"Yes," I said, giving him a smile. "Just looking at all of the faces in there, seeing if there's anybody I know."

"I can take it down to the library and get you a photocopy of it if you like it that much," he said.

"That would be great, Grandad, if you could?"

"No problem," he said. "I need to go to the library anyway, so I might as well while I'm there."

"I see that Grandma and Alice and Auntie Em are in the photo," I remarked, testing the water to make sure nothing else had changed.

"Yes," he chuckled, "just the same as yesterday."

I stopped then so I wouldn't drop myself in it; I didn't want my grandad to think I was going mad. My dad had always told me I ought to think more before opening my mouth to speak. Perhaps he was right!

After dinner, I got ready to leave.

"Thank you, Grandma. That was absolutely lovely, you make the best chips in the whole world."

"Yes, she's one in a million," Grandad said.

They shared an affectionate grin.

"Off you go, mate," Grandad said. "Have fun."

"I will," I said as I ran out of the door, slamming it behind me.

I went to Thomas's house and on the way Paul jogged up to meet me.

"Well?" he asked. "Is Aly in the photo?"

"Yes! Job done!" I told him. "Now, let's get Thomas and go to see if Auntie Alice is okay."

As we arrived, Auntie Alice was in the front garden, potting up some plants.

"Afternoon, boys," she said, "what brings you around here, George? I feel like I haven't seen you in weeks!"

I snuck a glance at Thomas and Paul, who all looked as pleased with themselves as I felt. Mission accomplished!

"Nothing," I said. "I just thought I'd pop around and see if you needed a hand with anything."

"That's nice of you!" she said. "Since you're here, you could help me move that pile of horse manure over into the corner of the garden."

She pointed it out and showed us where she kept her spades.

"You just had to ask, didn't you?" Thomas said, but he was still smiling.

We were all just so relieved she was alright.

Aunt Alice laughed. "Go on, boys. It won't kill you," she said and walked into the house.

"At least we know everything's okay, if she hasn't seen us for a few weeks," Paul said.

"It's like the pavement slabs," I said. "We changed the course of time when we took the medal back."

"Come on," said Thomas, picking up a shovel. "Let's get this over with."

"Yeah," I said. "We sort of owe her, anyway."

When we finished, Auntie Alice brought us all glasses of squash. "You'd better go in and wash your hands and then come out and get your drinks."

When we returned, she asked, "So, what brings you here? To what do I owe the honour?"

We told her that we were doing a school project and we were learning about the history of town and the shops in the new term.

"Yes," Thomas said. "Our teacher wanted us to pick a shop and then research it."

"Okay, I'll see if I can help you," she told us. "What shop are you researching?"

"We were wondering if you could tell us anything about the Co-Op?" I said. "We know you were there on the day it opened, because Grandad has a photo in the living room with you, Grandma, and Auntie Emma."

"Yes, I remember that day quite well," she said, with a smile. "It was a hot, beautiful summer's day during the school holidays. We were all there for the opening. It was like a carnival. The year the shop opened was 1936, and it was a big deal for the town as it was a large shop where you could buy lots of different things in one place. Unusual things, things you couldn't buy at the other shops in the town, like the butchers or the bakers."

"Did you always go down into town with your sisters?" I asked.

"Yes," she replied, "but it was safer then, so don't get any ideas. We also met up with our friends that day, but we had to be careful our parents didn't find out or we'd have been grounded for hanging out with boys." She frowned. "You know, I think my dad only went up there that day to try and see if he could find some boys."

"What boys?" I asked, with a grin on my face as I knew it was us.

"Just some boys from outside the village that me, your grandma, and Auntie Em made friends with," she said. "But in those days, boys couldn't hang out with girls. It was silly, really. What else can I tell you about the Co-Op?" she asked.

"Nothing," I replied. "We have everything we need!"

"But I've hardly told you anything about the shop," she said, surprised.

"That's okay, we have enough!" Thomas said.

"We're off to play on the rope swing now," Paul said. "Thanks for the drinks."

"Thanks for moving the horse manure!" She smiled.

"Bye Auntie Alice," Paul said cheekily.

Thomas grinned. "Yeah, bye Auntie Alice."

I rolled my eyes at them.

"Well," I said, when we were heading down towards the rope swing. "I think we've definitely done it - we've put history back to where it should be. Auntie Alice went to the Co-Op opening, she never fell out with her dad. We must have made sure he got the medal back!"

Later, when we were walking home, we ran into my grandad.

"Hello," he said. "Here."

He handed me a large, brown envelope.

"What's that?" I asked.

"A copy of the old photo from when the Co-Op was opened," he said.

Surprised, I looked at him and said, "Thanks! You didn't have to do it today."

"It's okay," he said cheerfully. "I had nothing else to do this afternoon! When you get to my age you look for things to do."

"Thanks again, Grandad!" I said, as he set off back towards the house he shared with Grandma.

"Why have you got that?" Thomas asked.

"Grandad said I could have a copy, since I liked it," I explained. "And then I thought it would be a good idea to keep an eye on it. That way, we can see if we accidently change anything again."

"Good idea," said Paul. "Where should we keep it?"

"Well, we can't take it back to the den," I said.

"Why?" Thomas asked.

"Well, for a start, this photo hasn't been taken yet back then, so if we take it back and anyone sees it, our secret will be blown," I told them. "Also, photographs cost a lot of money back then - money that we shouldn't have. Also, the plastic paper it's printed on didn't exist in 1936."

"Oh, yes!" he said. "Well, how about I look after it for the moment?"

"Why not George?" Paul asked.

"I don't have any nosy brothers who might go looking for it - and if we need it on the day of your grandma's funeral, we won't be able to look at it if we give it to you."

"Cool, then we can look at it every day when we get back, in case we change anything," Paul said.

"Hey, if the girls are going to be away for a few more days, why don't we spend tomorrow investigating the second magic door?" I suggested.

They both agreed, with much excitement. We couldn't wait to find out when we'd end up this time!

Chapter Sixteen

New Adventure

"Morning you two," I said, at half past eight the next morning. "Are we all ready for a day of adventure?"

"Oh, yes!" said Paul.

I kicked off the wall I'd been leaning on, enjoying the sunshine.

We all wore massive grins as we walked down towards the quarry. After some discussion, we decided it would be safest to travel through the new door in stages, as we had with the first one. Not only did it mean that Paul and Thomas would be safe, in case something happened, but also that they'd be able to see me come and go, so we could pinpoint the exact location of the second magic door.

"Are you sure you're happy to go through on your own?" Thomas asked.

"Yes," I said. "This time I'll just pop my head across and have a look, then come back."

When we got down to the water's edge, we sat on the bankside where we'd been throwing stones a few days before.

"Is this where you were?" Paul asked.

"Yes," I said, showing him exactly where we'd been. "I threw the rock and then a couple of minutes later it just came flying back."

"That must have been really weird," he said.

"You're telling us!" Thomas laughed. "I nearly had a heart attack! Must have been worse for whoever threw the rock, though - at least we know what's going on."

"You probably scared somebody half to death," he said, laughing.

We grabbed some rocks and threw them in different parts of the quarry pool to see if any of them disappeared.

I threw the first one, but it just hit the water with a splash. Thomas followed and then Paul, until we were all just throwing stones into the water and having fun. We'd quite forgotten what we were looking for.

Just then, I threw a stone and it disappeared.

"There!" I said. "It vanished!"

"That's where I threw my stone," Thomas said, frowning, "but mine splashed."

"Okay, then!" I said. "At the same time we both need to throw a stone at exactly the same place and see whether our stones go through."

"Ready?" said Thomas, as we both picked up rocks.

"Ready," I said. "On three. One, two, three!"

Sure enough, Thomas's hit the water with a splash while mine went through.

"Well, there it is for sure!" Paul said. "Only George's rock can go through, just like it's only him who can go through on his own."

"Okay, then," said Thomas. "But how can we get to it in the water? It's too far from the wall to walk through and I don't feel like swimming in there. It's far too deep."

"What are we going to do?" Paul asked.

"Yeah, we can't swim all that way, we'll drown," I agreed. "How about this? My dad told me how to make a raft the other day!"

"A raft?" Paul asked.

Thomas looked interested. "How we can make one of them?"

I told them how my dad and his friend used to make them and play here on the quarry.

"His mate showed him how to do it," I told them. "We need to get an old door from the allotments and four car wheels!"

"Wheels?" Paul asked, looking at me as if I'd lost my mind.

"Yes, wheels," I said. "Still on their rims, with air in them. Then you float the four tyres together on the water and put the door on top, tie some rope around the whole thing, and that's it."

"Okay, but where do we get four tyres from?" Thomas said.

"Doesn't your grandad have some old wheels in his garden, by the shed?" Paul asked.

He was right! "Yes!" I said, surprised. "He used to have an old Mini, but when he got rid of it, he kept the wheels. It drives my grandma mad, them being there doing nothing!"

"Alright, we'll go and see your grandad and ask him if we can have - I mean, borrow - the wheels," said Paul.

I nodded.

"Do you really think he's going to let us take the four wheels?" Thomas asked.

I had a funny feeling that he would, since he was usually pretty good like that - unlike my dad, who would have had a fit because he'd know exactly what we were up to.

So, off we went, up to my grandad's.

"What are we going to tell him we want the wheels for?" Thomas asked.

"We can tell him we're going to make a car," I said. "He'll buy that story, I'm sure."

"Morning, boys," he said, when he answered the door. "What can I do for you today?"

"Hi, Grandad! We're making a car and we've noticed that you've got some spare wheels in the garden, by the shed."

He nodded. "Yes, they're off my old Mini. I've been meaning to get rid of them."

"So, you wouldn't mind if we borrowed them?" I asked hopefully.

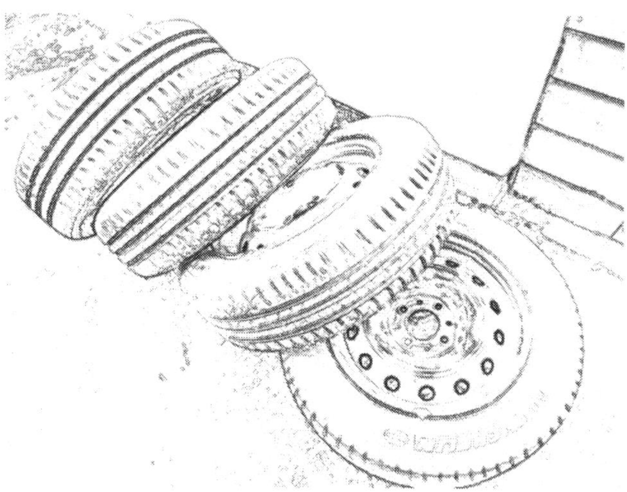

"You can keep them," he said. "Just don't dump them anywhere. You'd be doing me a favour - and you'd be putting me in Grandma's good books. She's been nagging me to get rid of these wheels for years, but I knew they'd come in handy for somebody, sometime." He grinned at us. "But if you think I'm hauling these through the house you've got another thing coming!"

We laughed with him.

"Go around the back and get the tyres and I'll help you throw them over the gate."

So, one by one we grabbed the tyres and rolled them up to the gate.

"How are we going to do this, then? There's three of us and four wheels," Paul pointed out.

"Here," said Grandad, carrying an old metal bar. "Put the wheels on this. It should be long enough. Then you can carry them all together."

"Thanks, Grandad," I said. "I'll bring it back later!"

"It's okay, mate!" he said, ruffling my hair. "You can keep it."

It was hard work, carrying the tyres, and although we set off quickly, we soon slowed down. Even with all three of us carrying it - me at the front, Thomas at the back, and Paul switching places with us when it got too heavy - we got very tired.

At the quarry, we decided to hide the tyres in the long grass and put some fallen branches over the top so no one would discover them while we went up to the old allotments to find an old wooden door for our raft.

When we found an old door acting as a fence panel we all looked at each other and smiled.

"This would be perfect!" I said. "We need to be careful we don't get caught, though."

"If we take this, it's stealing," Paul pointed out.

"Stop worrying," Thomas said dismissively. "If it bothers you that much, we'll bring it back when we're finished." He laughed and told Paul to shut up.

We knew it was wrong, but it was a bit of a thrill, borrowing the door. As luck would have it, the door was just resting up against the fence posts, so taking it away was very easy.

"Let's quickly get it down to the water before anybody sees us!" I said.

"What about the rope?" Paul asked.

"We could get it from the rope swing," I said.

"There was enough left over from when we made it," Thomas added.

We sent Paul off to go and get it with Thomas's penknife, while Thomas and I took the door back to the quarry. We put it beside the water's edge, then grabbed a wheel each and started bringing them over to the door. By the time we got all four wheels down by the water, Paul was getting back with the rope.

"Got it," he said, running over. "What next?"

Now came the tricky part. Somehow, we needed to put the wheels in the water and then lay the door on top of them, all without falling in.

As Thomas leant forward to drop his wheel in the water, he lost his balance and nearly fell in. I had to grab him by his belt and pull him back.

"Be careful, Thomas. You don't want to be the fourth person drowned in the quarry," I said.

As I said it, the wheel that was already in the water started to float away.

"Quick!" I said. "Grab the pole and use it to stop the wheel floating away."

Thomas did as I suggested.

"That's it," I said. "You've got it. Now, move it slowly this way."

As it got closer Thomas put his hand out and started to pull a wheel closer, but he lost his grip on the pole, which slipped through the centre of the wheel and into the water.

"I've lost your grandad's steel," he cried, grabbing onto the wheel. "Sorry."

"Don't worry about it," I said. "Grandad said we could keep it, so he'll never know we lost it."

"That's just as well, then," Paul said, laughing. "Because I know I'm not going in there after it."

Carefully, we floated all four tyres alongside each other in a rectangle close to the bankside, then carefully slid the door over the top of them.

I gingerly climbed on the door.

"Careful," said Paul, passing me the rope.

"Yeah," I said.

I was putting on a brave face for my friends, but after Thomas's near-slip the story of the boys who'd drowned in the quarry was in the forefront of my mind as I passed the rope under the water and around the tyres, then pulled it back around to the top of the door to secure them.

"That's a good sign," Thomas said, when I was done. "At least it floats. That's a good start, well done."

I handed them the loose end of the rope - there were several feet of rope left. "Come on, then! Pull me along - but not too fast; I don't want to go in."

The raft was behaving beautifully. As long as they had a weight on top of the wheels, they wouldn't float out from underneath! It was perfect. I was glad my dad had told me how to do it.

After pulling me back towards the bankside where we started, Paul asked, "How are you going to get through the magic door? You need to power it somehow!"

"I don't know," I said. Looking around, I spotted a long, flat piece of wood I could use as an oar. "Here, pass me that old piece of wooden plank."

Thomas pulled it out from where it had been lying, half out of the long grass.

"Well, here I go," I said, making myself comfortable on the raft.

"Are you nervous?" Thomas asked.

"About what?" I asked. "Falling off and drowning, or going through the second magic door? Because the answer for both is yes!"

We all laughed, mostly out of nerves.

"Is there enough rope that you can keep hold of it, so that when I go through the door you can still pull me back?"

"Yes, I think so," said Thomas. "We should be okay, but we'll soon find out!"

"Okay, this is it," I said. "When you see me disappear, if you haven't seen me for more than three minutes, pull back gently on the rope."

"Yes," Paul said. "Don't worry, I'll keep an eye on my watch. We've got you."

"Well, it's been nice knowing you." I laughed and gave them a wave.

Kneeling on the raft, I started to slowly paddle towards the magic door. The more I paddled, the more I realised I had to move the paddle from one side to the other in order to go in a straight line through the water.

I was paddling hard and was beginning to make good progress. My shoulders began to hurt, but I pressed on. I kept looking behind me and as I got close to where I thought the door was, I called over my shoulder, "Can you still see me?"

"Yes!" Thomas shouted back.

"Here I go, then!" I shouted as I paddled the rest of the way through.

As I passed the horizon where the door hung in the air, the air around me abruptly stopped moving. By now, this was a familiar sensation, so I knew this was it: I was moving through the door. As I got to the other side, I lay flat on the raft and looked back over my shoulder. Thomas and Paul had gone from on the bank and where they'd been standing now looked completely different.

I knew then I had passed through another magic door into another time, but when? I laid flat on the board for about ten minutes. I could see that the rope was still attached to the raft and was stretched through the time door, so I could only assume they still had hold of the other end of it. Time must have been passing differently on this side.

I looked around to see what I could make out and the quarry looked more or less the same; like in 1936 the trees were different, but this time I thought I recognised the positions of some of the smaller trees. Of course, they were bigger in my time.

I decided I was probably somewhere between our time and the girls' time.

The first tug on the raft took me by surprise and I nearly slid off the front of it; I had to hold on tightly. As I was pulled back through the door I watched the more familiar trees in front of me go from small to suddenly bigger. It was as if I was passing through a haze, then the sky turned from grey to blue.

Somewhere behind me, I heard Paul shout, "Are you okay?"

"Yes!" I shouted and gave them a wave. "Pull me back in."

I climbed off the raft when I reached the bank. To my surprise my legs were a little wobbly.

"What was it like, then?" Paul asked. He was bouncing up and down in excitement, like a small puppy.

I told him what I'd seen on the far side.

"How long were you in there for?" Paul asked.

I looked at my watch. "Ten minutes. How long was I out here for?"

"Just the one minute," he said.

"Wow, that's a much bigger time difference than the other door!" I said.

"Yes," said Thomas. "We'll need to remember to bring food through with us, or we'll starve to death!"

We all laughed.

Building the raft had taken quite a long time, so we decided to hide the raft and come back later. We pulled it over to the corner of the water, near the long grass, and tied it to a tree so it couldn't drift across the pool. Then we covered it with bushes to keep it safe, ready for tomorrow's adventure.

"That's well hidden, nobody's going to be able to find that," I said as we walked to the village.

On the way home we discussed what to do the next day; we had to decide which magic door to go through. Since the girls were away for a few days, it made more sense to us to explore the new door a bit more. But how?

The raft was only really big enough for two of us to travel over at once, and - like before - Thomas and Paul probably needed to be close to me in order to pass through the door, particularly given that Thomas's stone hadn't gone through the door when he threw it.

"First we have to see if you both can go through on your own," I said. "If you can't, I'll have to take you one at a time, leave one of you there and then come back to the other."

"No," Thomas and Paul both said very quickly and together.

"There's no way you're leaving me there on my own," Paul said. "What would happen if you drowned on the way back, or the magic door closed? No, absolutely not. We need to come up with a better plan!"

We walked quietly for a few minutes, thinking.

"We could try to make the raft wider by either getting a larger door or by adding planks of wood to make it bigger," I suggested. "Then we could all go through together."

"Then that's what we'll do!" Thomas said, sounding relieved.

We arranged to meet at 8:30 the next morning and then went our separate ways.

When I got into the house, Mum and Dad were sitting on the settee in the living room, watching TV.

"Evening, George. Where have you been?" Dad asked.

"Just down the rope swing with Thomas and Paul."

"You three spend a lot of time at the rope swing," he said. "I don't want you getting bored and being tempted to go to the quarry, because like I said, it's far too dangerous."

"We won't," I lied.

Dangerous - he doesn't even know the half of it! I thought.

"I don't want to play down the quarry," I told them. "Apart from the water there's nothing down there for me!"

"That's good to know," said Mum.

"Dad," I said, sitting on the rug, "I know you told me your friend George drowned down the quarry back in 1966, but do you know what happened to the two boys back in 1936 who drowned?"

"I know one of them was a friend of your auntie Alice and your grandma," he said, "and the other boy was a friend of his, but they didn't ever find out who he was." He sighed. "I'm sorry I don't know any more than that. You need to ask them about it if you want more detail. I do remember Mum saying that they saw them both fall in and go under the water. They never came back up. There was a big search party from the village and the police spent days looking for them, but they never found their bodies. Just like my friend George.

"If you want to learn more about the boys you should talk to your grandma, Em, or Alice," he said. "But promise me that whatever you do, you won't play down there! I don't want to have the police knocking on the door and telling me you've drowned!"

"I promise," I said. My fingers were crossed behind my back.

"You can go around and see them now if you like, and take this cake tin back for me," said Mum, getting up to fetch it.

I ran to my grandma and grandad's house and knocked on the door.

When it opened, Grandad said, "Hello again, mate! What can I do for you this time?"

"I've brought this cake tin back from Mum for Grandma."

"You'd better come in, then," he said. "Your Grandma is in the middle of baking a cake with Alice."

I walked into the kitchen, enjoying the smell of cakes baking; it pulled me into the kitchen like a magnetic force.

"Here's your cake tin, Grandma," I said. "Can I stay while you and Auntie Alice bake?"

"Why not? You can sit there and we can chat, if you like."

I hopped on a kitchen chair and watched them work, cleaning up from the first part of baking and preparing to decorate the cake once it had baked. Grandma and Auntie

Alice moved around one another with practiced ease born of years of familiarity.

"Grandma," I said, "can you tell me about the two boys who drowned down the quarry, back in 1936?"

Grandma and Auntie Alice stopped what they were doing and shared a look.

"Why?" she asked, surprised.

"Well, Dad told me about his friend who drowned in 1966, and told me to ask you about the boys who drowned when you were little." I tried to come up with a reason to be asking about something so morbid. "It's all to do with this school project we're doing, learning about the history of the village. The quarry is on the list of things to find out about, too."

Grandad, who'd been doing the crossword at the table, stood up and said, "I'll get some drinks." He walked over to the fridge to grab some bottles of cola.

Auntie Alice took a seat at the table beside me.

"When we were about your age, we used to play at the quarry and on the rope swing," she told me. "It was the same place your grandad tells me you have your rope swing, funnily enough. That summer we met some boys at the start of the school holidays, who lived a few villages over. Their names were Thomas, Paul, and George. Actually," she said, glancing at Grandma, "that's quite a coincidence, isn't it? I've never thought of that before - those are the same names as you and your friends!"

I took a glass of cola from Grandad, trying to hold back a smile. Little did she know that it wasn't a coincidence at all!

"We spent a lot of time with them that summer," said Grandma, smiling sadly at the memory. "We played on the rope swing, went into town together… they even had a sort of den over at the allotments. And they gave us the key!"

"It was very exciting," said Auntie Alice. "We weren't supposed to play with boys, and they weren't as mean as the ones we knew at the time. We got up to all sorts of mischief!" Her smile faded. "Then, one day, tragedy struck."

I felt a chill run down my spine. I wasn't sure I wanted to hear what she had to say, but I needed to know.

"Go on!" I said quietly.

"We saw two of our friends fall in and drown," she said sadly.

"It was awful," said Grandma.

Grandad put an arm around her shoulders.

"We all ran around the quarry, shouting for them, trying to see if we could see them, but there was nothing, no sign!" Auntie Alice said. "Our other friend stayed and carried on looking for them, while we ran up to the village to get our parents and summon help."

"The whole village turned out to look for them," said Grandma. "It lasted for days, but they never found the boys."

"And the same thing happened to your dad's friend, 30 years later," said Alice. "Even at the time I thought it was a horrible coincidence."

"It was tragic," Grandma said as she wiped her eyes dry. "We missed our friends very much - and so did your dad, later on."

Grandad gave Grandma a proper hug, then patted Alice on the shoulder. I thought he must have been sad, too, but didn't want to show it.

Despite this, they still didn't tell me not go down to the quarry. Not even Auntie Alice.

Grandma said, "When you're playing down the quarry… firstly, don't get caught by your dad, or none of us will ever hear the end of it. Secondly, you have to be very careful of the water, because although it's hot weather at the moment, the water in the pool is so deep that it's ice-cold. If you fall in, the shock that hits your body will stop you from being able to swim your way out."

"That's why it's so easy to drown if you fall in," Auntie Alice added. "And however good a swimmer you think you are, if you fall in the water you will most probably never come back out!"

"I'll be careful, I promise," I said.

This was one promise I intended to keep.

"Right," said Grandad, clapping his hands. "No more talk about the boys who drowned. Let's think of the fun you girls had when you played down there with your friends instead. I bet you were great at that rope swing, Iris."

For a little while, we chatted about the adventures Grandma and Auntie Alice got up to when they were children - many of which I'd already heard.

"Well, time's getting on now," Grandma said, looking at the clock. "You should go home. I'll pop some of these cakes in the tin when they cool and you can come and pick them up tomorrow, if you like?"

"Okay Grandma," I said, "but I might have to try one before I take them home, just to make sure you're not trying to poison my mum and dad."

We all laughed.

She rubbed my shoulders and gave me a kiss on my forehead before saying, "Of course! There will be an extra cake for you for when you get here. Now, off you go and we'll see you tomorrow."

"Goodbye, Auntie Alice," I said as she kissed me on the forehead.

"Goodbye," Grandad said as he shook my hand. "See you tomorrow."

I couldn't wait to tell Thomas and Paul about the story I'd just heard from Grandma and Auntie Alice! It was far too late to talk to them that night, though. So instead I went home and spent the rest of the evening wondering which of us was going to be the one to fall into the water at the quarry and never be seen again. We would have to be very careful to make sure none of us really drowned.

After breakfast the next morning I went to call on Thomas, and when he came out I told him about the conversation I'd had the evening before.

"But I need to tell you and Paul together," I said.

Something of my concern must have been written on my face because Thomas looked curious and somewhat worried at this. When we got to Paul's house and knocked on the door, his mum answered.

"Hi, boys. Paul can't come out today, I'm afraid. He's coming with us. We need to go and see some family before the funeral."

"When do you leave?" I asked.

"We'll be leaving in about half an hour, so if you want to go indoors and see him, he's upstairs," she offered. "But don't distract him, we need to get ready to go."

Thomas and I both went in the house and ran up the stairs to his room.

He was sitting on his bed, packing a backpack when we went inside. He looked up at our expressions and immediately said, "What's wrong?"

"George has something to tell us both!" Thomas said as he closed the door.

I filled them in on what Grandma and Auntie Alice had said about the boys who'd drowned in 1936.

"Who do you think it was?" Paul asked. "One of us?"

"I don't know," I said. "We have to make sure none of us fall in, especially when we're using the raft!"

"Given that we need the raft to use the other magic door, should we just scrap it?" Paul suggested. "Then we know we'll be safe."

"I can't," I said. "Do you remember what my dad told me about his friend who died? I think that was me. He said he got hit in the head by a rock that came out of nowhere. I bet that was us, the other day."

"Did he throw it back?" Thomas asked, astonished.

"Yes. He also told me the boy that drowned saved his life. So, I don't think we can ignore the second door, because I think if we don't go through, my dad will fall in the quarry and I will never have been born."

"Wow," said Paul.

"Yeah," I said. It was a strange thing to contemplate. "I'll try to make sure I don't fall in and drown this time. It should be easy now that I know what's going to happen."

"Yeah, but what if something goes wrong?" Thomas asked.

"Grandma told me the water's so cold under the surface that when you fall in you can't use your arms and legs properly, so people panic and go under. I'll be able to stay calm and try to straighten out, so I'll float, then I'll compose myself and swim out."

"Who do you think the boys were that your aunts and grandma saw drown?" Paul asked.

"I don't know," I said. I had been wondering the same thing. "They didn't use names, but I know it wasn't my dad. So two of us are going to get in trouble in 1936."

"That's not good," said Thomas, who looked a little pale.

"The only way for you both to be completely safe is to only let me go through and save my dad," I told them. "That way we can be sure that no one ever drowns, but it means breaking our laws by going alone and splitting up."

They both tried to change my mind about going on my own, but they knew deep down that it was the right thing to do to keep them both safe. I was a little worried about what might happen to me, though, if I got into trouble and they weren't there to help.

"I'll go through a few times to become his friend and try to find out what date his friend drowned."

"I won't be able to come down to the quarry with you any more until after my holiday," Paul said. "We have to go and see family today and tomorrow, ready for the funeral. Then we go away, so this might be the last time you see me before I get back. Promise me you'll both be careful! I don't want to come back to find you're the boys who drowned."

A dark look passed between us.

"Promise," I said.

"Me too," said Thomas.

Paul's mum shouted us all down as they needed to get on the road.

"I have to go now," Paul said.

"Well, if we don't see you before you go on holiday, have a great time," I laughed.

Paul shook my hand. "Bye, then. Good luck saving your dad!"

He shook Thomas's hand, too.

We went down the stairs and left the house, saying goodbye to Paul's mum and dad as we went.

"What should we do?" Thomas asked.

"Well, the girls won't be back until tomorrow, so we could go through magic door number two for a look around," I said. "We know nobody will drown today because Aly and Iris won't be there to see it, so it must happen after they get back."

"Okay," he said, "but first we need to make the raft a little bit wider and make a paddle each so we can get across the water more quickly and easily."

"We could ask Grandad for some when we go to see Grandma to get the cakes I need to pick up. We could even take a cake when we go and see the girls, tomorrow," I said. "I bet they'd like that."

"Yeah," Thomas said and laughed. "We could tell them we made them. That would be funny."

We went and got Patch (who needed a walk) from Thomas's on the way to Grandma's house. When we got there, Grandad had all the doors and windows wide open, as it was a very hot day. I could still smell the freshly baked cakes as I got to the gate.

"Hi Grandma, hi Grandad!" I shouted through.

"Hi George," she said, "come on in!"

"I have Thomas and Patch with me, is it okay if they come in?"

"Of course it is," Grandad shouted from inside, "bring my favourite dog here!"

"I suppose you've come for your cake?" Grandma said, with a smile.

There was no fooling her; she knew I couldn't resist her cakes.

"Yes, please," I replied.

"Just as well I left two cakes out," she said as she passed us one each.

"Look at your grandad," Thomas said, grinning. "He's like a big kid with that dog."

"Den, will you leave the dog alone?" she laughed. "I think you think more of him than you do of me!" She shook her head and turned to me. "The cakes I cooked for your mum and dad won't be ready to pick up until tomorrow," Grandma said.

"That's okay, I'll grab them tomorrow," I said, "but if you have a spare one for Thomas and me that would be lovely. We could have a picnic with it."

"I'll see what I can do," she said, smiling. "Is Paul not going to be with you?"

"No, it's the funeral tomorrow, and then he goes away on holiday," said Thomas.

As we were finishing up our cakes, I casually said to Grandad, "Do you have any spare planks of wood and nails?"

"Yes, I have loads in the shed, just help yourself."

"About time," Grandma said. "I've been nagging him for years to empty that shed, and you're doing it for him, thank you!"

When we looked in the shed we found just what we needed to make the raft wider. We saw some home-made paddles too.

"That's handy," Thomas said as he grabbed a handful of wood and the paddles.

Unbeknownst to us, Grandad had followed us out. "If you do go down the quarry just promise me one thing - be careful and don't fall in," he said, making us both jump.

"Okay, I won't. I promise," I said. We both grinned at each other and he gave me a hug.

"Grandad's the best!" I said, as we walked away.

"I know," said Thomas. "Even though we play down the quarry, he doesn't mind, he just tells us to be careful. I wish my dad was like that."

With all we needed in hand we grabbed the dog and I said, "We're off now! I'll see you tomorrow to pick the cakes up!"

Thomas dropped the dog back off at home and we made our way down to the quarry to make the raft bigger and safer, so we could both use it at once.

When we got down there, the raft was still where we left it, undisturbed.

"It's still here," I said.

"I told you this was a good place to hide it."

We dragged it along to the water's edge, out of the grass where we could work on it safely, and started nailing the planks on top of the door. We'd forgotten to get a hammer, so we used a rock to hammer in the nails Grandad had given us.

"That should do it!" I said, as we sat back to admire our work. "It looks sturdy enough, now, and big enough for two."

Very carefully, we both climbed on top of it, steadying ourselves as it wobbled from side to side.

"Steady," I said. "We need to sit low down. You stay behind me."

As we started to balance the raft, we put the paddles in the water and started moving it slowly along the bankside.

"This isn't as hard as I thought," Thomas said as we paddled it around the water.

Within a few minutes we had learned how to keep it stable and how to move it in any direction. If we needed to turn left we'd put the paddles on our right, and if we wanted to turn it right we put the paddles on our left. To go forward we had one paddle on either side - simple!

"Okay, then," I said. "Are you ready?

"As ready as I'll ever be!" Thomas replied, with a nervous tremor in his voice.

"Okay, it's now nearly 1 o'clock. Look at where our shadow is now and see if it's the same on the other side - at least that way we'll know then if it's 1 o'clock there, too." I said. "Did you leave Paul's watch under the rock?"

"Yes," said Thomas. "Let's go before anyone sees us."

"Here goes!" I cried. "A new adventure awaits."

Carefully, we both started paddling towards the second magic door and, with a quick look around us to make sure nobody was watching, we paddled through to the other side.

CHAPTER SEVENTEEN

MEETING A NEW FRIEND

"We're here, whenever that is," I said as we paddled the raft around, away from the middle of the water and towards the other bankside.

"We need to pull the raft up and hide it for now," I said.

"Let's put it over there," Thomas said, "in the same place we hid it in 1986!"

The grass was just as long and overgrown in this time as in ours.

As we were covering the raft with bushes, I heard a boy yelp.

"Help! I'm falling!"

I turned to see a boy clinging onto the quarry wall.

"Look, Thomas!" I shouted, as I ran towards the boy. "Hold on!"

We raced around the quarry wall and I flung myself on the grass above where he was hanging. Then I reached down and grabbed him by the arm.

"Hold on!" I said. "I've got you. Grab my belt, Thomas!"

Together, Thomas and I pulled him back up the wall and a little way away from the water's edge.

"Are you okay?" I said. "That was close."

"Yes," the boy said, as he brushed himself down. "I thought I was going in that time."

"That time?" I repeated. "How many times have you nearly fallen in?"

"Loads," he said, managing to sound offhand. "I'm trying to see if I can build a rope support from one side of the wall to the other."

I looked at him. This was clearly my dad - he even had the same nose, and the cut on his head from where my stone must have hit him - but here he was, going out of his way to put himself at risk.

I just had to ask, "But why?"

"I don't know," he said, shrugging. "Just because, as far as I know, it's not been done, so why not?"

I didn't have an answer, but I kind of agreed with him. It sounded like a fun idea, but I had to remember what my Grandad had said and the conversation with my grandma and my auntie Alice. After all, it was usually Dad trying to make me be sensible. I owed it to him to try to change his mind.

"Yes," I said out loud, "but I think it's a bit silly putting yourself at risk for such a stupid reason."

"You're starting to sound like my dad," the boy said and laughed. He reached out to shake hands with both of us. "Hi, my name is John, John Rainbow."

Thomas grinned at me; I could hardly keep the smile off my own face. This was definitely my dad.

"Haven't I seen you down here before?" John asked.

"I don't think so," I said.

I hadn't travelled properly through this magic door before, though I did see him through the door over the water, which meant he must have been able to see us through it too. *Could he be able to travel through the time door like me?* I thought to myself.

We played together around the quarry, throwing stones into the water and climbing trees, for about an hour or so, soon becoming fast friends.

Eventually he said, "I have to go now. I need to go shopping with my mum, but thanks again for helping me out there!"

"No problem," I said with an excited grin on my face.

"Will I see you both tomorrow?" he asked.

"Maybe," I said, but Thomas nudged my shoulder.

"We're meeting the girls tomorrow," he reminded me.

"We could do both," I said. "We might see you tomorrow," I told John.

"Well, I'm down here most days," he said. "If I see you, I'll see you. Goodbye and thanks again!"

We watched him run off towards the village.

When he was gone I said to Thomas, "I need to sit down. I can't believe what just happened!"

"I know," he said. "You're telling me. That must've been the story your dad told you about when someone called George saved his life."

"No, it couldn't have been that," I said. "My dad said they were friends and got up to loads of fun before I fell in and drowned."

"Don't say it like that," he said, pulling a face. "It freaks me out to think you could die here. And why would you be here on your own with him and not with me?" he asked.

"Remember," I said, "it's too dangerous for you to be here, just in case you're the one who falls in and drowns.

He told me the boy drowned the day after Pamela's birthday and that's next week, a few days after the fair."

Thomas nodded thoughtfully. With no more said we went off to the oak tree to see our names carved into it, and when we got there I saw a rope swing tied to the top branch. I laughed and pointed it out to Thomas.

"This must have always been a rope swing tree, for every generation."

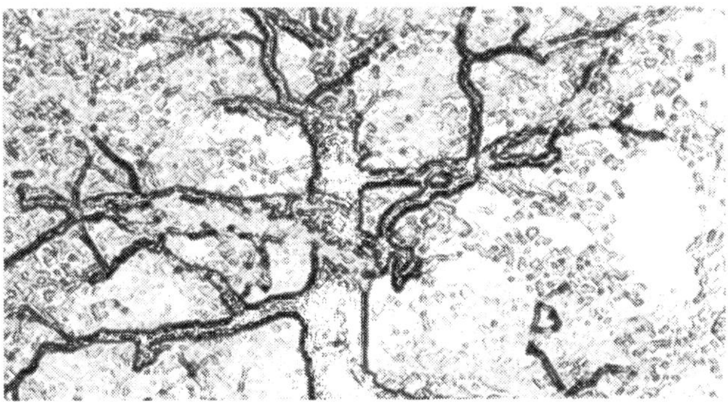

"Let's have a go, then," Thomas said, grabbing the rope and running out as fast as he could over the water.

We both played on the swing for well over three hours. Eventually, our arms began to ache and I suggested that we should go up and see if our den was still in the allotment.

"Okay," Thomas said.

We ran off towards the allotments. Although we were just normal kids we felt like the luckiest kids in the world. We were time travellers! It was incredible to be able to travel backwards and forwards to different times.

At the allotment, we rushed up to our plot.

"There it is!" I said. "It looks a little bit tatty, but the den's still there and half the greenhouse glass is intact."

"Do you think anybody used it after us?" Thomas asked.

"It doesn't look like it; it's all overgrown."

We decided we should sneak in, but not through the gate on the main path. Instead, we went around the side and snuck in through a hole in the fence at the back.

To our surprise, our original padlock was still there, but the latch that held it to the door was broken off. We had a quick look around and when we saw there was no one there we quickly went inside.

"This is strange," I said as I looked around. "We were only here yesterday and it was brand new, now it's got holes in the ceiling, a broken window, the floors are rotten, and our wooden stools are just broken down pieces of wood with dried bark around them."

"You're not wrong," said Thomas.

I looked around and said, "If nobody's using this allotment - and to be honest, it looks like there isn't, by the state of it - we could still use this as our den in 1966."

"Yes," he agreed, "but it's a little bit scruffy and rough-looking."

"I know," I said. "But how about when we go back to 1936 we take some of the money Grandad gave me and buy some wood paint or something and protect the wood, so it lasts longer? Then when we come back to now it should be in much better condition."

"Sounds like a plan," he said. "Let's get out of here before we get caught, and in the meantime we can work on a plan for making it last longer."

It was getting on towards 7 o'clock in the evening so we needed to start thinking about going back.

"It should be about 2 o'clock back home if the time difference is 10-to-1 here," I said.

"Okay," I continued, on the way back to the quarry, "in order for us to get back through the magic door we need to go in the opposite direction to when we went through earlier, so we need to paddle around to the other side of the water and then come back through this way, just the same as we do on the other magic door."

"Why?" Thomas asked.

"Well, we still don't know what happens if we go through the same magic door in the same direction twice," I reasoned. "So we must always go through it in one direction and then come back in the opposite direction, just to be sure. Otherwise, who knows where we could end up!"

We climbed onto the raft and paddled slowly towards the magic door, looking around. We couldn't see anyone about.

"We have to be careful when we paddle through that nobody on the other side in 1986 can see us," I said. "So, we need to go through as slowly as possible, and if we see anybody we need to paddle backwards!"

"Okay," Thomas replied.

Warily, we approached the door.

"Carefully does it!"

I was at the front and therefore first to pop my head through to 1986.

"The coast is clear," I said, and we paddled through. "We're back in 1986!"

We both let out a sigh of relief; after all, this was the first time we'd travelled back through magic door number two without a tether.

As we got to the bank we both climbed off the raft and tied it up. "Go and grab the watch, Thomas," I said. "See what time it is."

Thomas came back with the watch. "It's 1:45 p.m. by Paul's watch. What time do you make it?"

"7 o'clock, according to my watch."

"That's definitely about 1 hour here to 10 hours there, then!" I said, doing the calculations in my head.

We dragged the raft over to our hiding place and buried it again in the bushes.

"Come on, then," I said, "let's go home for lunch - I'm starving!"

On the way back to the village we stopped at the allotments and leant on the fence.

"I'm looking forward to going back tomorrow to buy the paint and do this place up, so it's still intact in 1966," I said as we gazed at the dilapidated pile of rotting timbers where our den had once stood.

"Just think, if we make a really good job of it in 1936 and then tidy it up again in 1966, it might even still be here now."

"I suppose you're right," he said. "We'll have to wait and see."

We carried on towards the village and home.

"Same rules apply," I said, when we reached the end of our road. "We must only ever go through one magic door once per day."

"Agreed!" Thomas said. "We'd be too tired and hungry to do it more than once."

After lunch, we both played at the rope swing until the evening drew on, talking about our new adventure in 1966 and meeting my dad.

"Are you going to ask him any more questions about his friends when you get home tonight?" Thomas asked.

"Are you kidding?" I said, excited. "I can't wait!"

"It's getting on now," Thomas said, jumping off the swing. "I have to go in."

"Me too," I said. "I'll see you here tomorrow morning at 8:30 - but don't forget we've got to grab the cakes from Grandma's house so we can take one back for the girls!"

"I won't forget," he replied. "See you tomorrow."

As usual that summer, when I walked in the house I had a big grin on my face.

"What are you looking so happy about?" Dad asked.

"Nothing," I said as I jumped on the settee next to him, laying my head on his arm. "Just had a really good day playing on the rope swing and building a tree house."

I realised I'd done it again: I'd lied. And it had come out so naturally it made me feel so bad.

Ignoring my feelings, I asked, "Did you ever play on a rope swing when you were my age?"

"Oh, yes," he said. "Down by the old oak tree, where you built yours. We used to swing right out over the stream and play for hours."

"Who with?"

Of course, I knew it was with me and Thomas, but I wanted to hear him say it.

"Me and my friend George and occasionally his friend, Thomas."

That was the first time I'd heard my dad mention Thomas's name; before now he'd always referred to him as 'George's friend'.

Was it possible that we'd changed the past by going back and saving Dad, which meant he met us both?

"Did you play with both of them?"

He went on to tell me, "I only really played with Thomas on a few occasions, but I didn't see him much. I did see him occasionally across the water with some girls who I think were George's friends, too. However, when George drowned I never saw them again and they never helped look for him or joined the search party. It was strange."

That must mean Dad can see through the magic door, then. How interesting, I thought to myself.

"Was he not there on the day that George saved your life?"

"No," he said. "Unfortunately not. If he was, maybe George wouldn't have died."

Again, as Dad spoke of his friend I saw him getting a bit upset. It really must have affected him.

He rubbed his eyes, "Come along, then. Time for bed."

Chapter Eighteen

Future-Proofing the Den

The next morning was beautiful, as every day that long summer had been. I left the house with a reminder from my mum to pick up the cakes from Grandma and Grandad's house and then went to meet up with Thomas.

As I got to his door he came running out. He was so excited.

"I can't wait to see your grandma today!"

"Well, that's okay," I said. "We're going to see her now."

"Er… no, not your grandma now!" he said, laughing, "Iris and her sisters in the past, silly."

"Come on, then, let's go and see Grandma and Grandad," I said. "I need to get the cakes for mum, but remember we need to keep one to take to 'Grandma' in 1936!"

"It sounds funny, saying that you're going to get a cake from your grandma to give to your grandma," Thomas said.

"I know. It's bizarre."

Outside their house, Grandad was sitting in the yard with a handkerchief on his head, enjoying the morning sun.

"Morning boys, what are you up to today?" he asked. He smiled, but he didn't lift his head from where it was resting on the back of the chair.

"First I have to take some cake home to Mum and then Grandma said we can take a spare cake, so we're going down to the rope swing for a picnic!"

Just then, Grandma came to the door. "Your cakes are all ready," she said. "They're on the table in the tins. The three big tins are for your mum and this square blue tin is for you two."

"Thanks!" said Thomas.

Thomas and I went into the kitchen to grab the four cake tins, while Grandad just sat there sunbathing on his lounge chair, enjoying the morning's fresh air.

"I'll take these over to Mum now," I said. "We're off, thanks again for the cake!"

As we were about to leave, Grandma said to us, "Are you sure you don't want to take Grandad with you?" She laughed.

Thomas and I looked at each other, as if to say no, and for so many reasons we couldn't tell them.

"Stop being silly, Iris," Grandad said, sounding comfortable. "You boys run along and have a good day. If you go down by the quarry, be careful," he added in an undertone, smiling.

We took the three cakes home first and then set off to the quarry.

We were looking forward to seeing the girls as we hadn't seen them for a few days. Thomas kept saying how he couldn't wait to give Iris the cake, knowing that she'd baked it only yesterday.

"Just remember," I said, "my grandma is still a 60-year-old lady!"

Thomas laughed. "I know," he said. "I'm just saying I'm excited to see her. Stop panicking, I don't fancy your grandma!" He shuddered and laughed. "It sounds so weird when I say it like that."

We went to the rope swing and put the tin in the vault, then I looked at my watch.

"It's only 10 o'clock," I told him.

"We've got loads of time before going through the magic door, if we can't go through until 1 o'clock," Thomas said.

"Yeah," I said. "I'd like to do something fun, though."

"I know," Thomas agreed. "We should only go through at 1 o'clock to know where we are, but we're here now. So, why don't we go through and see your dad and play with him for a little while? We would have all day there, then come back here and have lunch, then be able to go through and see Iris and the others?"

"We could, I suppose," I said, biting my lip, "but that would be breaking one of the laws."

"Yes," he said, "but we're only going to one time each per day, so we're not likely to bump into our other selves!"

Excited, he waited for my response.

"Okay, then," I said slowly. "I suppose it couldn't hurt when you say it like that. Let's do it."

We ran over to the water where the raft was hidden, then got it and ourselves ready for another exciting adventure with Dad back in 1966.

We got on the raft and started to make our way through the magic door. Then, with a quick look around we slowly paddled to the other side.

"We're here," I said, when we were through. "Let's hide the raft and go look for my dad."

"George, Thomas!" we heard John shout from behind us. "Where did you two just come from and what is that you're on?"

"It's a raft," I said as we paddled over towards him.

"That's really good!" he said, impressed. "How did you know how to build one of them?"

"My dad showed me," I said as Thomas and I climbed off it.

I showed John how it was constructed, and how it worked.

While he was examining it, out of his earshot, I said to Thomas, "I've just shown my dad how to build a raft and he then tells me how to build this raft in the future! How weird is that?"

We both laughed.

The three of us played for hours on the raft, taking turns and being careful not to pass through the magic door. After using it and getting a bit wet we decided to play at the rope swing and in the woods. We had an amazing day, but finally John had to go home. We both said goodbye and let him walk off, making sure he was completely out of sight before we went back to the raft to travel back to 1986.

It was strange to think that Dad was running home to get his tea from Iris, when we were going to take a young Iris a cake from the old Iris. It boggled the mind.

We paddled the raft to the bank and dragged it out, concealing it in the bushes. When we checked our watch we found we had been consistent; we'd only been gone for about 45 minutes.

I said to Thomas, "If you like, I could take you through to 1936, leave you with the girls, and then come back to 1986 so I can travel to 1966 to see Dad sometimes.

Dad said he could occasionally see you and the girls across the water, so we must have travelled in two times on one or more occasions."

"Isn't that breaking one of our laws, though?" Thomas asked.

"What harm could it do?" I said. "As long as we don't go back to the same time zone on the same day, we'll never risk bumping into our other selves."

"I suppose so."

We went back to the oak tree to grab the cake, then made our way towards magic door number 1.

After a quick look around, we counted "3, 2, 1!" and walked through the door.

We went straight to the allotment, where I said, "We need to put the cake away and count up some money so we can go to the shop and buy some food. I'm absolutely starving! We need to do that before the girls get here!"

"Come on, then," he said. "I'm hungry, too."

As we made our way towards the allotments, I sighed, turned to Thomas, and said, "This is your fault!"

"What?" he replied, looking puzzled.

"That!" I said, pointing over towards the open gate on the allotment, where I could see Aly through the glass of the den window. "The girls are in our den. I think they think it's their den as well."

"You're not bothered, are you?" he said.

"No, of course not. That's my grandma, after all, and she looks after me and feeds me cakes. I'm just messing with you."

We both looked at each other and smiled. Neither of us could wait to give Iris the cake she'd made.

We went through the gate and walked towards the den, but we must have been spotted because the door opened before we got there.

"Morning, boys," Iris said as she pushed the door wider for us to come in.

"You're both here early," she said. "We weren't expecting you this early. You don't mind us being here, do you?"

"No, not at all," Thomas replied before I had the chance to speak.

"What's that you've got under your arm, George?" Aly asked.

"It's a cake that my grandma baked me. She said it was for me and my friends to share," I said as I handed it over to Iris, trying not to laugh.

"There you go, you can take care of the cake."

Thomas and I both had huge smiles on our faces.

"What are you both smiling about?" she asked suspiciously. "What have you done to this cake?"

"Nothing," I said, honestly. "It's just a cake."

"Let's have a slice, then!" Aly said.

When we opened the lid we found that Grandma had already cut the cake into eight slices.

"That's handy," Iris remarked. "Seeing as we don't have a knife down here." She grabbed a slice and handed the tin to Aly.

After she and Em took a piece, Thomas and I grabbed a slice each and we all started tucking into it. We watched Iris's expression, anticipating her reaction.

"Mmm," she said. "This is beautiful! Who did you say baked it?"

"My grandma, she likes baking cakes." I smiled.

"It's really nice," she replied. "Your grandma's a good cook!"

I nodded and asked, "Do you bake cakes?"

"Yes, she does!" Aly replied on her behalf. "But nowhere near as nice as this one!"

"I'm sure after a little bit of practice, your cakes will start to taste just as good as this one," Thomas said.

He looked at me and smirked.

"What are we going to get up to today?" Aly asked, licking her fingers.

My mouth was full, so Thomas jumped in and told them that we needed to go into town and buy some materials for the den, like paint, paintbrushes, and roof felt.

"We'll come with you to help buy and carry it all back, if you like?" Aly offered.

"That would be a big help, thank you," I said.

Thomas suggested we could also see what else we could find while we were there as we needed to try to make it look like a boy's den again and not the girl's pad our friends were trying to turn it into.

We all laughed.

We grabbed some money and wrote a list of the things we needed, which I put in my pocket. Then we locked up the den and started walking towards the town.

"We also need to look after the garden, as we're supposed to be getting it ready for my 'uncle' - that's our cover story," I reminded them. "So when we're there we also need to buy some cabbage and carrot seeds, and things for the greenhouse."

"What's on your list?" Aly asked.

"Wood paint, a paintbrush, something for the roof, plant pots and tomato seeds, cabbage and carrot seeds, man stuff to turn our den back into a man's den..." I read aloud.

"Come on, then," Iris said, with a smile on her face.

She linked arms with Thomas and dragged him off. Thomas turned around and grinned at me. I mouthed the words, "That's my grandma!"

I thought to myself, *I'm going to get a photo of her as an old lady and keep pulling it out my pocket every time he looks at me.*

I suppose he can't do any harm, though, I thought. *Grandma doesn't marry my grandad for another 10 years.*

"I'm not linking arms with you!" Aly said. "No offence!"

"That's alright," I said. "I don't want to link arms with you, either!"

We both laughed and looked at each other.

"Just good friends?" I asked.

"Yes, good friends," she said.

We shook each other's hands.

This suited me for obvious reasons, but I think she must have looked at me like her brother or cousin, but she couldn't quite put a finger on why. There must have been some instinct that we were related.

On the way into town the girls told us about the big opening day and carnival for the Co-Op in a few days. The town people were going to have a big festival and fair in celebration. They were obviously excited to go.

I looked at Thomas and whispered, "That's where the photo was taken!"

"What photo?" Aly asked, overhearing us talking.

I quickly turned and said, "I've heard there's going to be a photographer there, taking photos of the shopfront with everyone standing in front of it."

"Well, no one told me about that," Iris said.

"Me neither!" Aly replied, looking excited. "If that's the case, I want my photo taken outside the shop!"

"Me too," said Em, "it would be nice to look back in the future and see ourselves there."

"You mean you weren't going to go into town to see the opening?" I asked.

"Yes," she said, "but only for the fair, not for the photo. I'll have to make sure my hair looks good and wear my best clothes. If do get in the photo, that would be great! We might even be in the papers."

I pulled a face at Thomas as the three girls chatted excitedly about the photographer. I pulled him to one side and said, "They were never meant to get their photo taken! They're only on the photo because we've just told them about it!"

"Yeah, but they've been in that picture since the first time we came back, so it can't have done any harm," he reasoned.

Every tiny little thing we did seemed to make a difference in the future.

"We need to be so careful," I said. "Whatever you do don't kiss my grandma or get too attached - you could affect my entire future!"

"Don't panic!" he replied. "I won't."

Around the town we noticed a lot of people about, putting up banners, bunting, and streamers ready for the upcoming festivities.

"Well," Aly said, "I don't know why they're going to this much trouble to open one store, but I can't wait to have our photos taken. Thanks for letting us know about it, George, or we would have missed out!"

"No problem," I said, with a shrug, hoping it really was no problem.

"Let's go over to the hardware shop and get what we need for the den and the allotment!" I added.

"Don't you mean the DIY shop?" Aly laughed as she linked my arm, pulling me towards the shop.

As soon as we walked in, the shopkeeper asked us, "What can I do for you fine bunch today?"

I pulled out the list and showed it to him.

"And some man-stuff to turn our shed back into a man's den!" I laughed as I looked at Aly. "We're looking after my uncle's allotment and he gave us some money to get it set up."

"Right," he said. "Wait there while I gather up what you need."

As he put the paint down on the counter the shopkeeper said, "Make sure you only paint this on the outside of the shed. Don't breathe in the fumes, and don't get it on your clothes. Now, how many paintbrushes would you need?"

"Five, please!"

"Five?" Iris repeated.

Em pulled a face.

"I take it you girls aren't helping paint the shed, then?" the man asked, grinning.

"No," she said. "We'll tidy up inside and start potting up the seeds while the boys paint the outside."

"Two it is, then," the man said to himself as he put three of them back.

"Something for your roof?" He thought for a moment. "You need bitumen. It's a thick, heavy paint you apply before attaching roof felt. It's a brand new material designed to stop water getting in through rooftops, and if you're going to use that you'll need another two paintbrushes, because bitumen and wood stain don't mix."

He picked up the list again.

"Now then, let's see here," he muttered to himself. "Cabbage seeds, carrot seeds, pots, plants, and tomato seeds. I can help you with all of that."

He turned and grabbed some packets of seeds from the shelf behind him.

"Pots are over there by the door. I suggest 30 pots and two… no, three bags of compost. That should be enough for a standard size greenhouse."

"Do you need any tools, or a watering can?" he asked.

"No," I said. "Some things were already at the allotment, so this will be it, thank you!"

"What about a wheelbarrow?" he asked.

"A wheelbarrow?" I replied.

"Yes," he said. "Not only for when you're back at your allotment, moving soil and compost about, but also for now. How else are you going to get all of this stuff back home? It's too heavy for you all to carry."

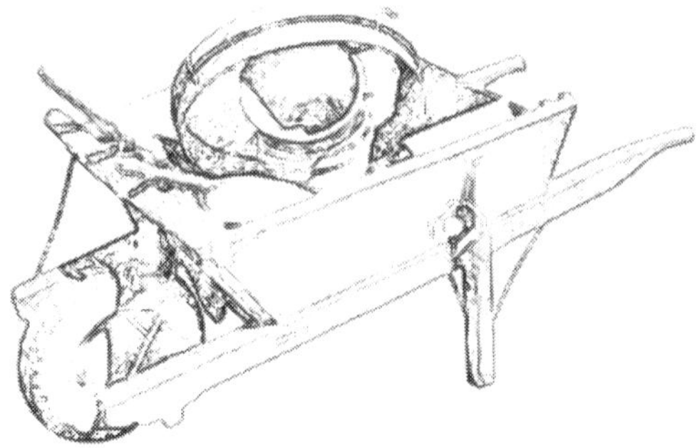

"Okay, then!" I said. "A wheelbarrow it is."

This guy wants us to buy the whole shop! I thought. But he was right. How else were we going to get everything back to the allotment? We hadn't got any food yet, either, and despite the cake, my stomach was beginning to rumble again.

The man took his pencil and a piece of paper and started to add up the cost.

After muttering to himself and scratching his pencil against the paper, and then looking out of the corner of his eyes as he was trying to do his sums, he said, "That will be £1 and 6 shillings!"

I looked at him and then looked down at my wheelbarrow full of stuff and thought to myself, *bargain!*

The only problem was I didn't know what six shillings meant. I flicked change around in my hand, pretending to add up, but Aly came to my rescue and took the correct change out my hand and then handed it over to him.

After getting some bread, cheese, meat, and some bottles of lemonade, we set off back to the den with our wheelbarrow full of everything we needed.

Iris linked her arm with Thomas's again and walked off in front, and next were Aly and Em, leaving me to push the wheelbarrow.

Thomas looked over his shoulder and asked, "You okay pushing that?"

"I suppose I'll have to be!" I replied, laughing.

"I'll give you a hand, if you like?" Aly said. "I'll help you push it halfway."

When we got back to the allotments, over an hour later, Aly had been as good as her word. She took the wheelbarrow from me at the gate and wheeled it down to the den. "I told you I'd help!" she said, grinning and laughing.

Luckily, I saw the funny side.

The girls went into the den with the food, while Thomas and I unloaded the wheelbarrow. We took the seeds, compost, and plant pots straight to the greenhouse, then left the rest in a pile outside the den and went indoors.

Thomas and I ate our lunch, sharing a little bit of it with the girls. Em had to go home to help her mum with the housework, but she seemed relieved not to have to get her hands dirty.

"What should we do first?" Aly asked.

"Why don't you and Grand- er… I mean, Iris!" I coughed. "Why don't you start putting the compost in the plant pots over at the greenhouse?" I said, all flustered.

"Grand?" Iris asked, amused. "Why did you call me that? I know I'm beautiful, but I'm hardly grand!"

She and Aly stepped out of the den to go to the greenhouse, laughing together.

"That was close!" Thomas said. "You nearly called her 'Grandma'."

"I know! That would have taken some explaining," I said. "She would think I was saying she was an old woman and batter me, or something." I laughed. "This time travel business is harder than you think. Sometimes I daren't even breathe without thinking I'm going to change something in the future!"

As the girls made a start in the greenhouse, Thomas and I decided to do the roof first. It seemed a logical way to do a job: start at the top and finish at the bottom.

We opened the tin of bitumen and looked at each other. "It's like treacle," I said. "How're we going to paint this on the roof?"

"I know!" he said. "We can just pour it on then move it around with the paintbrush to even it out, then we can lay the roof felt straight on top."

"Okay," I said, "sounds like a plan."

We grabbed a paintbrush each and made a start, and soon we'd managed to cover the whole roof using the entire tin of bitumen. Then we laid the felt over the top and nailed it down in the corners.

"Come on, Thomas," I said, "the girls don't look like they're finished yet, so we might as well paint the outside and get it out of the way."

With the two of us painting the den, it only took around an hour and a half, and just as we finished, the girls walked out of the greenhouse.

"That was very good timing!" Aly remarked.

"Just as we finish all the hard work!" I teased. "You got the easy stuff." I laughed.

"That's enough for me," I told Thomas. "I'm not doing any more today. I need to go and get cleaned up before I go home."

"Us too," the girls said, as it was time they got off home as well.

"We'll see you tomorrow?" we asked.

"Not me," Aly said. "I've got to help Emma tidy our bedroom."

"I'm not doing anything," Iris said. "I could meet you here?"

"Okay," Thomas replied, really quickly. "See you tomorrow. Say, 10 o'clock in the morning?"

"Yes," she said, as they ran off up the garden. "Looking forward to it already, bye now."

"What time is it, George?"

"It's 6 o'clock!" I replied. So that should make it around 2 o'clock back home, I think?"

"We should hurry, then," he said. "We need to get back home for lunch. I know we've already eaten, but we've spent a whole day in two different times. After all this hard work I'm famished - and we're already late!"

After getting changed, we walked up to the magic door and, making sure that no one could see us, we nudged up against each other and sneaked through.

On our way back up towards the village we stopped off at the old allotments.

"Look Thomas, the den is still there!" I said excitedly. "Only yesterday it was totally gone."

Pleased with our morning's work, we turned to head home to have our lunch. But just before we left, Thomas grabbed my arm. "Wait!" he said. "What's that over there in the old greenhouse frame? Look, under the bench."

"I don't believe it!" I said. "It's the square, blue tin Grandma gave us for the cake."

The tin was in poor condition: it was battered, dented, and the paint was flaking off, pitted with what looked like rust holes. It was definitely still the same tin Grandma had given me that morning.

"Should we take it back to your grandma?" Thomas laughed.

"Could you imagine?" I said and laughed as well.

We agreed to leave the tin there for now and then tomorrow put it under the bench in the den to see if it's in a better condition when we came back the following evening.

We played for hours on the rope swing that afternoon.

"I feel like I've been playing out for days, today!" Thomas said tiredly. "I bet I'll sleep tonight."

"Me too," I said. "Let's go home and get a good night's rest, ready for tomorrow."

We went our separate ways and arranged to meet outside my house at 9 o'clock the next morning.

When I got home I sat and talked to my dad for a little while before bed, asking him about the way the village was when he was growing up. I wanted to find out as much as I could before going back so that I could make sure I wasn't going to change anything in the future.

This was going to work; I knew it.

Chapter Nineteen

Splitting Up

At the quarry the next day, Thomas and I prepared to travel separately for the first time. It was a little daunting to think about, but I couldn't risk Thomas drowning in 1966, and the boys who drowned in 1936 wouldn't do so until after the carnival for the Co-Op, so he might as well enjoy himself in the meantime.

It was particularly important to make sure my dad - who seemed to be able to see through the second portal - didn't follow us through it.

"This is it," I said, as we approached the first magic door. "We'll go through to meet Iris and you can both go for a walk and sit on the bank. I'll travel back home and then back to see my dad in 1966 and look out for you. I'll wave if I do, and if you see me, you must wave back."

"What if Iris wants to come over and talk to you both?"

"You'll need to make up an excuse," I said. "I know, tell her that you don't like my friend John and that he's a troublemaker. Tell her that your dad has forbidden you to play with him, or something like that."

"Are you sure?" he asked. "I feel a little bad lying to her."

"Are you kidding me?" I scoffed. "This is all we do every day. Unfortunately, it seems like being a time traveller also makes you a liar!"

We walked through magic door number 1 and made our way towards the den.

"I'm nervous!" Thomas admitted, as we got nearer to the allotments. "I'm not sure how I'll feel being here on my own!"

"You'll be fine!" I said. "Don't panic, I'll only be 30 feet away from you," I added laughingly.

Shortly after arriving at the den, Iris came down on her own as she'd said she would.

"Hello, boys," she said brightly. "What are we up to today?"

"I'm going to pop over to see my friend, so you two will have to keep each other company," I said.

"That's fine by me," Iris replied, grabbing Thomas by the arm.

I rolled my eyes. "Remember she's my grandma," I mouthed at Thomas, when she wasn't looking.

"Right, I'm off! Thomas, you can see me to the gate!" I said. At the gate I told Thomas, "You need to be at the other side of the quarry by 10:30 a.m. and look out for me."

"How will I know the time?" he said.

I took my watch off, the one Grandad had given me.

Take this," I said. "You might as well keep a hold of it if we're going to start splitting up, but take good care of it as it means a lot to me. I'll take Paul's watch and keep it in my pocket."

"Okay," he said. "I'll tell Iris I want to go for a walk just after 10 o'clock. Goodbye for now and good luck," he said nervously, as he shook my hand.

I made my way down to the water, making sure nobody could see me. Then I took the raft from its hiding place under the bushes and started paddling across the quarry towards magic door number 2.

With a quick last look around I paddled slowly through the door and over towards the corner, where I planned to hide it for the day. It was harder getting the raft out of the water without Thomas's help and I'd just finished covering it up with the bushes when I heard John call my name.

"George! George! Over here!"

I looked across at the quarry wall, where I saw my dad sitting with his feet dangling over the edge. I ran over, excited to meet him again and spend the day with him.

"I thought you weren't coming down," he said.

"Well, change of plan," I said. "I thought I'd just come and see what you were up to."

"I've been in the woods, making a treehouse," he said. "But if you want to go down to the rope swing we could play down there."

I wanted to play, but instead I said, "We could sit here first for a little while and just enjoy the peace and quiet."

He looked at me funny, as if he thought I sounded like an old man, but I didn't care. I wanted to see if I could see Thomas and Iris.

We chatted for about 10 minutes before John noticed that I kept looking over towards the other side of the quarry, where I'd told Thomas and Iris to go.

"What are you looking at?" John asked.

I just told the truth. "I'm looking for Thomas and Iris!"

"Who's Iris? Thomas's girlfriend? That must be them over there," he said, pointing over to the other side of the quarry.

A chill ran down my spine as I saw Iris and Thomas standing on the water's edge, waving at me. Thomas had a smile stretching right across the whole of his face, knowing that we were right and the plan had worked.

I couldn't believe I was looking straight at Thomas while we waved at each other from two different times.

It was so exciting, but I knew it was dangerous. I knew we were playing with fire.

"Are we going over there?" John asked.

"No," I said. "I don't particularly like Iris. My dad told me I'm not allowed to play with her."

"Come on, then," he said, "let's go and play on the rope swing instead."

John and I played for hours on the swing and in the woods at his treehouse until the day drew on and it became late.

"I have to go home now," John said, "but I've had a great day. Thanks!"

"Me too," I said. "Same time tomorrow?"

"Absolutely," he replied with a smile. "Do you want to walk up together?"

"No!" I said quickly. "I need to look for Thomas and walk home with him."

He didn't question me and set off on his own.

I gave him five minutes to get away before I grabbed the raft and quickly paddled up to the magic door to travel back to 1986.

I'd only been gone for about 50 minutes in 1986, but I was starving. I'd been playing nearly all day in 1966. I couldn't go home to ask for any food because my mum thought I hadn't long had my breakfast, so I went straight to the magic door number one and passed through to 1936.

Once there, I ran to the den as fast as I could to grab a slice of cake. When I got there Thomas and Iris were already inside.

"Hello, you two!" I said as I grabbed a slice of cake and rammed it down my throat so hard I nearly choked.

"Calm down," Iris said, "you'd think you hadn't been fed all day."

Thomas laughed, knowing the truth; I really hadn't eaten all day.

I met Thomas's eyes and he took the hint. We went outside under the premise of checking the roof.

"What was it like?" he asked, making a show of examining the freshly applied felt.

"It was amazing," I said. "It was so unreal seeing you and Iris across the water. What did you do after you saw us leave?" I asked him.

He told me that they went to play on the rope swing for about an hour and then returned to the allotment for about an hour.

"That's weird!" I said. "While you were on the rope swing in 1936, me and my dad went to play on it in 1966! Just think, we were both playing on the rope swing at exactly the same time! How strange is that?"

I told Thomas that I wanted to do the same thing for the next few days. "I really want to get to know Dad before I have to save his life. I remember him telling me that we became the best of friends before I drowned, so that's what I must do."

"That's fine by me!" Thomas said. "I felt okay being there today with Iris. She made me feel comfortable and safe. You can spend all day there with your dad and you will only have been missing from here for an hour, so you can get the best of both worlds! Quite literally." He laughed.

Just then, Iris came out. "Are you both going to spend all day out here and leave me in there on my own?"

Thomas looked at me. "What should we do now?"

"Well, why don't we all go down and see Elsa?" I suggested.

"Elsa, why?" he asked. "Are you sure?"

"Well, there's no reason why we can't go over there and become friends. What harm can it do? We'll take Iris, then that's two girls and two boys, so no one will feel left out!"

"Okay," he said. "I suppose it can't hurt. Iris, do you want to come?"

"Where to?"

"Ash Meadows. My friend Elsa lives there," I told her.

"If you're both going then I'll come," she said, a huge smile on her face, grabbing Thomas by the arm again.

The walk would have taken us about an hour, but because we were both showing off and acting up in front of Iris it took nearly two hours. Eventually we arrived at the play area where we'd last spent time with Elsa.

"How are we going to find her?" Thomas asked. "We can't knock on the door because she's not supposed to hang about with boys."

"We could just hang around and see if she comes out," I started to say, but before I'd finished my sentence I saw her walking towards us.

As she looked up and realised it was Thomas and me she smiled and started skipping towards us.

"Afternoon," she said. "Hello, boys. And this is?"

"Sorry, where are my manners?" I said. "This is Iris, my gr- friend."

"What's a 'gr' friend?" She laughed. "Is she your girlfriend?" She shook Iris's hand.

"Oh no," we both said at the same time. "Just friends."

Thomas looked at me and rolled his eyes.

"You really need to be more careful," he whispered.

"Where's Paul?" she asked. "Is he still away on holiday?"

"Yes, and won't be back for a few days, so you just have us to put up with," I said.

She asked me to play on the swings with her. As we walked over to them we left Thomas and Iris by the seesaw.

The four of us played there for hours, having fun, laughing, giggling, and taking turns playing on everything.

It was nearing teatime when we heard Elsa's mum calling her name.

"I have to go," she said. "If my mum sees me here playing with boys I'll be in real trouble. Will you be here tomorrow?"

"Yes," we all said, together.

Iris told her that she'd have her sister Aly with her and they would both come and call on her.

"Great," she said. "I'm allowed to play with other girls, I'll tell my mum you're new to the village. I'd better go now, goodbye!" she called as she ran home.

"It's probably time we started getting back," Iris said. "It's getting late and I don't want to get into trouble or grounded neither."

The walk back took far less time as we were all tired; we made our way straight there without messing around. In the village, we walked Iris halfway home before she said, "I'd better go on my own from here, just in case I get seen with you both, but I'll see you at the den tomorrow, yes?"

"Absolutely!" Thomas said. "But George will have to pop away again for an hour, if that's okay?"

"Of course it's okay, I'm not your mum!" She laughed and ran off.

"No, she's not your mum, is she, George? She's your grand-mum!" he said and laughed really loudly.

It was time we were getting back home. I was absolutely starving; I felt like I hadn't eaten for days.

"We're going to have to go to the shop on the way to Elsa's tomorrow, or I'll end up losing weight!" I said. "I might go and ask Grandma if she has any more cake so I can take it and keep it in the den for when I finish playing with my dad."

I decided I would tell her we were having a picnic and hopefully she might make me some sandwiches as well.

We made our way up towards the village in our own time for some lunch, after which we popped over to Grandma and Grandad's house to ask if she had any more of that beautiful cake that we could take with us tomorrow to have a picnic with.

As always, when I got to their house, Grandma couldn't do enough to help and Grandad even suggested making the sandwiches without us asking.

"Just come back first thing tomorrow and it will be ready and packed up for you," she said.

"Thank you, Grandma," I said. "I'll see you around 9 o'clock, if that's okay?"

"No problem, sweetheart," she said as she kissed me on the brow.

"Goodbye," Grandad said, patting my back. "See you tomorrow, mate."

Chapter Twenty

Meeting Up

The next day, as planned, Thomas was at my door just before 8:30 a.m.

"Morning, George," he said. "Ready for another full day?"

"I can't wait!" I said. "Let's go to Grandma's and grab our packed lunch!"

When we got there, Grandad was already walking out of the door with the bag in his hand.

"Here you go, boys," he said, handing our picnic over. "All ready for your long adventure?"

When we left, Thomas asked, "What do you think he meant by that?"

"I don't know… I just don't know."

Thomas thought for a minute, before gasping. "Do you think your Grandad might be the man who grabbed your arm and saved your life?" he asked, eyes wide. "And the same guy who paid the allotment off?"

"I don't know," I said, shocked. "It could be possible! It could be that he's a time traveller too. He was pretty cagey about not answering any of our questions… No, no!" I said. "It's ridiculous! If that were true he wouldn't let us travel through time - it's far too dangerous. You're just letting your imagination run away with you."

"I suppose you're right," he said. "Just a thought."

As planned, when we got to the quarry we travelled back to 1936 so Thomas could meet up with the girls and arrange to go over and see Elsa later that day. Then I went back to 1986 so that I could go through magic door number 2 to meet up with my dad and get to know him better.

We continued to do this for a few days. By now we thought we were expert time travellers and that nothing could go wrong or spoil the fun we were having. We felt like we were the luckiest kids in the whole world.

I was getting to know my dad like never before. We got up to all sorts of mischief - exactly the sort of thing he told me not to do in my own time. Meanwhile, Thomas was enjoying his time with Iris, and all three of us were enjoying going to meet Elsa over at her village. Everything was perfect.

Elsa became really good friends with us all; when we played together she would always link my arm with hers, like Iris did with Thomas. I don't know if she was just copying Iris, like kids do, but it didn't matter to me. I enjoyed her company.

I didn't want the school holidays to ever end, and to be perfectly honest, with the time differences in each world, at this rate it felt like they never would.

On the day before the carnival, after leaving John in 1966 (having had a full day of fun), I went and met up with Thomas, Iris, and Aly. Em was at home, as usual.

As I walked towards the den, they were walking out. “Ready for another day, you three?” I asked.

“Yes,” Aly said as she grabbed me, adding, “I'd better make the most of you before we meet up with Elsa! She'll want your arm back.”

She, Iris, and Thomas teased me about liking Elsa all the way to Ash Meadows.

When we got to her village, Thomas and I waited down on the swings, while Iris and Aly called on her. The only thing that could have made our time better was if Paul was with us. Thomas and I couldn't wait for him to get back from his holiday.

The girls all came over shortly afterwards and we played for hours, having fun, laughing, joking around, and making the most of each other's company. We'd all become great friends and things were looking good.

As usual, I was really tired and hungry; living almost two days at a time was beginning to take its toll.

“It's time we went, I think,” I said to Thomas.

“Yes,” Iris replied. “It's getting late and we've got to get home.”

“Will I see you all tomorrow?” Elsa asked.

“No,” I said. “We have to go to the town fair, but you're welcome to come, if you like.”

I was thinking to myself, *Please say yes, please say you'll come.*

But sadly, she didn't. “So sorry, I can't,” she replied sadly. “I won't be allowed.”

Aly told her not to worry and that the fair wasn't on all day, so we could see her afterwards.

“Yes, please do,” she said. “If you wouldn't mind.”

"Of course not," I said, thinking to myself that I'd like to spend as much time with her as I could.

She was a great person and really good company.

Off she went towards home as we walked off in the opposite direction. At the same time, Elsa and I looked over our shoulders at each other and smiled. We kept looking back at one another until we were out of sight. I felt a real connection with her; it was so exciting.

"Somebody fancies Elsa," Aly said, grinning and throwing her arm around mine. "Come along, then," she added, "before you decide to stay down here forever!"

I think she was a little jealous, not because she fancied me, but because Aly was a close friend to Elsa and she didn't want to lose either of us to another friend. Little did she know, she would never ever lose me; Aly would be my friend forever - I just couldn't tell her.

Shortly afterwards, we reached the village.

"We'll go from here," Iris said. "We don't want to get caught with you, especially this close to the fair. Imagine getting grounded now? That would be so disappointing. I'm really excited to go there and have my photo taken!"

"Remember, though, boys, if you see us with our parents, don't come and talk to us," Aly reminded us. "We'll look out for you and catch up when they've gone."

"I think Father said we're going for around 11 o'clock in the morning, so look out for us," Iris added.

The girls both went off and Thomas and I walked down towards the quarry.

"That's okay, then," I said to Thomas. "If we aren't meeting them until 11 o'clock down town, we don't need to leave the den until 10:30, which means I can go and see my dad for the day before we go. I haven't got long to spend with him before I save his life. At our age, anyway."

"When is it you save his life?"

"The day after the fair," I said. "It's my auntie Pamela's birthday tomorrow and I save his life the day after that."

"You can't come with me on the day I save him," I continued. "You need to be on the other side of the quarry with Iris in 1936 to keep an eye on me."

"You think that they didn't see two separate drownings?" Thomas asked, surprised. "You think the girls saw what happened through the door over the water?"

"Remember, Grandma told us the story," I said. "She saw us fall in - she must have meant me and Dad. We can't change the past by changing what we do."

"Yes," he promised. "I'll always have your back, even if we are 30 years apart."

I told him that we'd be fine and that I'd been rehearsing what to do when I fell in. "I'll just flatten out, hold my breath and compose myself, then swim to the middle and swim down, out of sight! Then I'll pop through the magic door back to 1986, where he can't see me. He needs to think I've drowned."

"Doesn't that seem a little cruel?" Thomas asked. "Letting him think you're dead?"

"I know, but that's the timeline. We can't change anything - and besides, if he doesn't think I'm dead, my name might not be George when we get home and I might have never have found the magic door if we were all allowed to play down there."

"I suppose it makes sense when you say it like that!" he said. "You need to save him, but you can't change the future.

I get it." Thomas pondered for a moment. "So, what will I do tomorrow, when you're in 1966 with your dad?"

"Well, if you wouldn't mind staying in 1986 for a bit and then just walking around the quarry looking for me, see where you can see us from?"

"Okay," he said. "I suppose it'll only be for a few hours before we have to go up to the fair."

"Great, then it's a plan," I said.

"Yes, good plan!" he replied, as we both stepped through the magic door back into 1986.

We made our way home, and as we got towards our houses we both said goodbye. Thomas told me to make sure I got a good night's sleep as I had a long two days ahead of me tomorrow.

We both laughed.

When I walked into the house, my grandad was sitting on the settee with my dad.

"Hello, mate," Grandad said.

"Hello, Grandad, what brings you around here?" I asked, wondering whether he knew what we were up to.

"I just came to see your dad and my favourite grandson."

David and Sean both rolled their eyes and carried on watching TV.

It was unusual to see Grandad around our house; we would normally always go to his, and he was acting strange and looked worried.

"What's wrong, Grandad?" I asked, jumping on the settee next to him. "You don't look your normal happy self?"

"Nothing," he said. "Just having a bit of a down day and I thought I'd come and see my mate to cheer myself up." He put his arm around my shoulder and pulled me into a hug.

We sat and watched TV together for a while, until my dad said it was time for bed.

"Good night, Grandad," I said.

After my bath, I lay in bed and couldn't stop thinking about what Thomas had said about my grandad possibly being a time traveller. Why was he here, tonight of all nights? And why did he look so sad? I fell asleep with these questions running around inside my head.

After breakfast, as planned, Thomas was waiting outside my door for 8:30.

"Ready for a new day and new adventures?" I asked.

"You bet," he smiled.

We quickly made our way down towards the quarry, all excited and ready for the day.

On the way we went over the plan we'd discussed the night before, and when we got down to the water we both moved the bushes from the raft.

I climbed on board. "I'm off now. Once you see me disappear, walk around the quarry until you can see me, then mark the spot."

"Have fun!" he said, as I started paddling out into the middle of the water.

I took one last look over my shoulder at him before paddling through the door; he waved and then disappeared.

After a quick look around on the other side to see that no one could see me, I paddled the raft back over to the corner of the quarry.

"George!" I heard John shout. I turned and looked up.

"Hello John!" I shouted and waved as he ran up towards me.

"Where did you just pop up from?" he asked. "One minute you're not here and the next you are."

Thinking fast, I said, "I just came through the woods today and not across the field!"

"Okay then, whatever you say," he said, though I'm not sure he believed me. "I've managed to borrow a rope from my dad's garage. I want to tie it across the wall and see if we can't make it the whole way across the wall front. What do you think?"

What I was thinking was that this wasn't supposed to happen until the next day, so I needed to come up with a plan to stop him from doing it today.

"I think I saw a policeman walking around the woods on my way up," I said. "I think it would be a little risky doing it today. Why don't we do it tomorrow and just hang out around the quarry today?"

"Okay," he replied as he threw the rope down. "We'll do it tomorrow."

I couldn't help thinking, *was I the one who encouraged him to do it tomorrow and therefore created the situation where I fell in? Was he was always supposed to do it today and no one drowned? This time travel is becoming very complicated.*

Nonetheless, I turned to John and said, "We need to just hang about here."

"Why?" John asked.

"I'm looking for Thomas. He might be down here soon."

To kill time we threw stones into the water, and just like with my other friends we competed to see who could throw their stone the furthest. Just as I was about to throw one of the biggest, heaviest stones I could find, I spotted

Thomas standing on the opposite bank, waving both arms above his head frantically.

John looked over and said, "Look, there's Thomas. Is he waving at us? He looks worried - do you think something's wrong?"

I looked at John and said, "I don't know. Maybe."

To my absolute horror, David and Sean ran into view and right up to Thomas.

"John!" I shouted. "Get down!"

I pulled him down into the long grass.

"Who's that?" he asked.

"They're my brothers and my dad told me that I can't play down at the quarry. If they see me they'll tell him and I'll be grounded for the rest of the summer holidays. I have to go back, now, John," I continued, "but we need to sneak away. I can't get caught."

John was fine with this, as we both crawled on our bellies away from the magic door.

"I'll see you tomorrow, yes?" he asked, when we were safely hidden amongst the trees.

"You can bet your life on it," I said, as I shook his hand and walked off.

As John ran off in the other direction I pretended to be walking towards the woods. I then grabbed the raft and paddled over towards the magic door. I knew there was a chance that Sean and David were still talking to Thomas, but I thought if he had any sense he'd try to convince them I'd gone down to the rope swing. They were stubborn and interfering enough to check.

Either way, I knew I needed to get through the door as quickly as possible and try to find out what they saw and how much they knew.

I carefully paddled through and, sure enough, they were gone. Relieved, I quickly paddled the raft over to the corner of the quarry, where I buried it with the bushes.

As I made my way over towards the rope swing, I heard Sean and David asking where I was.

"I'm here, what do you want?"

"Where have you been?" Sean demanded. "And who was that other boy you were playing with?"

"I went for a wee," I lied, hoping they wouldn't push me on it. "Not that it's any of your business! Come on, Thomas," I said. "Let's leave these two here."

"We know you're up to something," Sean said angrily. "Something's going on and we're going to find out what it is. We'll follow you all day if we have to, but we *will* find out!"

Thomas and I ran up towards the quarry as fast as we could, then dived down into the long grass by the magic door.

We crawled through so they wouldn't see us and wouldn't be able to follow us.

"Come on, we need to go to the den so I can have a heart attack in peace!" I laughed, but I was only half joking.

Safely ensconced in the den, we started talking about what had happened. Thomas said that he could see John and me as clear as day from the position he was in, but only from that position.

"And then, as if from nowhere, Sean and David came running up, asking where you were." He sighed. "That's why I was waving my arms to try and get their attention. I knew when I saw you duck down in the grass that you needed the opportunity to come back, so I told them you were down by the rope swing."

"Good thinking," I said. "I thought that's what your plan was. I hate to say it, but I think time travel is becoming too dangerous," I said. "I'm starting to think that we were only supposed to have this unique gift to help save my dad's life. I'm thinking after tomorrow, when I save him, we shouldn't come back."

"What about Iris, though?" Thomas asked, sadly.

"It was good while it lasted," I said, "but we can't risk getting caught or changing the future; it's just too dangerous."

I could see in Thomas's face that he was upset about this and didn't really want to stop time travelling, and to be perfectly honest neither did I. I quite enjoyed going to see Elsa.

"After the fair today I'm going to see Elsa to say goodbye," I told him. "Are you coming with me?"

"Yes," he said. "I want to say goodbye to her, too. Paul is going to be devastated when he comes back and finds out he's never going to see his grandma again!"

"I know," I said, "but it can't be helped. Come on, let's start making our way down town to see the girls and try to enjoy the fair!" I grabbed a handful of money from our tin and left the den.

On the way up to the allotment, we saw all three girls standing at the gate, waiting for us.

Thomas ran over, a big grin on his face. "I thought we were meeting you there?" he said to Iris, as they linked arms.

"We thought we'd surprise you," said Em, who seemed happy to see us again.

"So, we told our parents we'd meet them there," Aly added.

I must admit, I was just as excited as Thomas to see them. Aly and Em linked their arms with mine and we made our way into town.

CHAPTER TWENTY-ONE

THE TOWN PHOTO

After an hour of larking about, having real fun with the girls, knowing that this would probably be one of the last days we saw them, we started to approach the town. Distantly, we could hear music playing through an old fairground organ.

I was so excited. This was a real adventure, being back in time at a town fair and mingling with all the people as if we belonged.

The closer we got, the more voices we heard and the louder people sounded. We heard the fair people shouting, "Roll up, roll up! Knock the coconut off to win the prize!" as well as various other calls.

The town was bustling with people, all laughing and joking and smiling, queuing and taking turns to have a go at the coconut shy and hammer throwing competitions, or just standing and listening to the organ.

We joined a queue of children impatiently awaiting their turn on the merry-go-round.

"This is great, I can't believe this is happening!" I said to Thomas.

"Where's your dad?" Thomas asked Aly.

"I don't know," she said, "but he'll be up here soon, so if you feel me and Em just pushing you away, don't be offended. It means we've seen him and you can't be seen with me." She laughed and I nodded.

Finally our turn arrived on the magnificent, steam-powered merry-go-round. The horses were laid out in groups of three.

"We'll all go in front!" Iris declared. "You both can go behind on the inside two. That way, if Dad sees, he won't realise we're together!"

As we reached the operator, he put his hand out. "Halfpenny each!" he said.

I passed him a penny for Thomas and me. "Would you girls like me to pay for you?" I asked.

"No, thank you," Em said. "We have our own money, but thank you all the same."

As we rode on the merry-go-round we were all laughing and having a lot of fun. I made sure to keep an eye out because I was sure my great-grandad was on his way; I half expected to see him every time we went around.

As the ride started coming to a halt the music went quiet and I said to the girls, "I think your dad's over there."

"Where?" Iris asked, looking worried.

"Over by the hardware shop," I said. "I saw him with his dog!"

"Alright!" Iris said. "We'll go and play on the coconuts. He won't go over there; that's too much fun for him!"

The girls laughed.

All five of us ran, laughing and giggling, to the coconut shy. We were all excited to see if we could win a prize.

"What's the prize?" I asked the man behind the stall.

"Knock all three coconuts off to win a coconut," he said sarcastically.

I handed him my halfpenny for three hard wooden balls and I went for it.

My first ball missed the coconuts altogether, my second ball hit the stand the coconuts were standing on, and my third ball hit one of the coconuts square in the middle and bounced off, nearly hitting me on the rebound.

"That must be nailed on!" I said, laughing.

We all had a turn, each one of us trying to win a prize, but none of us could.

"There's a surprise!" Em remarked. "I don't think anyone ever wins on them. I'm sure they're fixed onto the posts!"

Thomas and I weren't bothered about winning. We were just having so much fun being at the fair without our parents, with a pocketful of money and with our new friends - in the past.

"There's a fortune teller's tent!" Aly said happily.

"Oh, great!" Iris replied. "I love those old fortune tellers. Let's go in."

The five of us walked up to the caravan. Iris pulled back the cloth door and looked inside.

There was an old lady sitting in the corner at a table, swathed in shawls. "Come in!" she said, in a calm, slow, Irish accent. "Sit down and make yourself comfortable."

As we went in, we all looked at each other, staring around at the general gaiety of the place. The caravan was full of hanging chains with jewellery attached to them. There were tapestries hanging on the walls and there was a colourful, patterned carpet that made you feel welcome. There was a strong scent of perfume or incense in the air.

I looked at the others and said, "That's handy, she has five chairs. She must have known we were coming."

We all laughed.

The lady pushed a tin over towards us with some pennies in it. "Well, I don't work for free!" she said, as we all dipped our hands in our pockets and dropped a penny each into the tin.

Without saying a word, we all sat down. The old lady leant forward in her chair and started waving her hands over a glass crystal ball.

"George!" she shouted with a screech, looking up at me with sinister, intense eyes. She grabbed my arm tightly. "You have travelled far, but you're not alone, and I see danger ahead."

I looked across at Thomas in total shock.

"How does she know?" I mouthed at Thomas, but he shrugged.

"You are being watched - watched by a strange man. Be wary!" she said. "Be very wary."

Abruptly, she sat back in her chair and closed her eyes. "You all should leave! You don't belong here!

We all went outside. "Well, that was a waste of money!" Iris said. "And you're not from that far away - only about a mile!"

She and her sisters laughed, but Thomas and I did not. The fortune teller had badly frightened us. Who was this stranger watching us? Could it be the same man who we now suspected was my grandad?

"There has to be some truth in it," I said to him, while the girls watched the organ. "She knew my name."

"What's the matter with you two?" Iris asked. "You don't believe her, do you?"

"I don't know," I said, unnerved. "How did she know my name?"

"She probably knows your dad from the village and is just playing you," said Em. "You know what fairground people are like!"

I nodded and exchanged a look with Thomas. Only he and I knew this couldn't be true.

Just then, we heard someone ringing the school bell. It was a call for everyone to come and have their photo taken outside the Co-Op.

"That's it!" Aly said, grabbing her sisters' hands. "They're about to take the photo!"

"Come on, then," Iris said, pulling Thomas by the arm.

Aly, Em, and I all ran behind them.

As we got close to the Co-Op, Iris said, "We can't stand there with you. You'll both have to go and stand at the other end, or Dad will know we're together."

We let the girls get ahead and then separated; they went to one end of the gathering crowd, while Thomas and I went to the other.

"Are you okay?" Thomas asked.

"No, I'm worried about the old woman and what she said about being in danger," I told him. "And I still have to go back to save my dad tomorrow."

"I'm starting to think you were right when you said we need to stop time travelling," he admitted. "It's becoming far too dangerous. Once you save your dad, that should be it. Well, at least for now?"

"Yes," I said. "We just have to be extra careful between now and then."

Just then, we heard the photographer tell everyone to look forward for the picture.

We both stood there, proud as punch, chests out and heads high, waiting for the flash.

It came with a puff of white smoke. We couldn't wait to get home to see ourselves in it, though we hadn't been in it before.

"I want to go and see Elsa now, before we go home," I said. "So we need the girls to move away from their dad, so we can go and ask them if they want to come."

Careful to stay among the busier parts of the crowd, we watched my great-grandad stalk around with his girls and his dog, until finally disappearing in the direction of the butchers, which his brother-in-law owned. As soon as he was out of sight, the girls came running over.

"Thomas and I are going over to see Elsa," I told them. "Are you coming?"

"We can't," Em said. "Dad wants us to walk back to the village with him, but when we get there we can play out later on if you like?"

Thomas turned and looked at me, whispering, "If this is one of our last days together, I want to spend as much of it with Iris as I can. Do you mind if I go to the den and meet them and we can catch up later?"

"Okay," I said. "I'll go over to Elsa's now and meet you back at the den in a few hours. Will you be okay walking back to the den on your own?"

"Yes," he said. "When I get there I'll do some gardening and pot some plants. The girls can look after them once we've gone."

Loud enough for the girls to hear, he said, "Okay, Iris. I'll walk a little bit behind you, being sure not to be seen, and meet you at the den. George is going over to Elsa's now and will meet us at the den later."

"Alright," Aly said, and they left us to meet their dad at the butcher shop.

"I'll hang about here," Thomas said. "Remember what the lady said - we're not here alone and we're being watched. Keep your eye out for anyone looking suspicious!"

We shook each other's hands and went our separate ways.

As much as I wanted to go and see Elsa I also wanted to be with Thomas and the girls, because I was a little scared and I wouldn't feel safe until I was back with them. I didn't blame him, though, for wanting to stay with Iris because I felt the same about Elsa.

Squaring my shoulders, I set off towards Ash Meadows.

Chapter Twenty-Two

It All Goes Wrong

I walked as fast as I could towards Elsa's house. I wanted to spend as much time with her as possible, as well as learn as much about her as I could so I could tell Paul all about her. He wouldn't be able to come and meet her again. It was too dangerous.

Subsequently, I arrived at the village a lot earlier than Elsa was expecting us. When I went to the play area she was nowhere to be seen, but it was still early. I couldn't wait all day for her to turn up, so I thought I'd walk down towards the house and see if I could see her.

When I got to her house I stood at the gate, looking to see if I could see her anywhere. To my surprise, I saw her running down the path.

"George, what are you doing here?" she asked, looking worried. "You know you're not supposed to be here until later on! If my mum sees us I'll be grounded. You shouldn't have come to the house, I'll get into so much trouble!"

She was angry with me. I winced.

"Sorry, Elsa," I said. "I had to come. Something's happened and I need to go away. I won't see you, ever again."

Her face fell, reading the truth of it from my expression. A tear rolled down my cheek.

"What do you mean you'll never see me again?" she asked. "What's going on? Tell me! I need to know."

"I can't, it's too complicated and dangerous, but I want you to know that I really like you and I've enjoyed spending time with you," I said. "But after today I have to go!"

Both of us were crying now and holding hands.

"Elsa!"

We both jumped. Her mum was calling her back in.

"I have to go," she said. She released my hand, turned, and walked away.

"Who was that you were talking to?" I heard her mum snap. "Get here! Get here, right now!"

There was so much I wanted to learn from her, so much I wanted to say, but I'd lost the opportunity. I was devastated. All I could do was watch her mum drag her into their house by the scruff of her neck.

I ran up the street, crying. I couldn't believe it was the last time I'd ever see her ever again. Time travel was too dangerous and too upsetting. For the first time I wished I'd never found the magic door at all.

Sadly, I made my way towards our village so I could meet up with Thomas and the girls at the den. I needed my friends around me, now more than ever. I almost ran the whole way and when I got there I was absolutely exhausted. Thomas was there on his own.

"What are you doing here so early?" he asked. "You're supposed to be spending the day with Elsa."

Tearfully, I went on to tell him what had happened. He was really upset for me.

"Where are the girls?" I asked.

"They're not here yet, they must still be with their dad," Thomas said.

"Should we go home and get some lunch, then?" I asked. "We can come back later on today?"

"Doesn't that break one of the laws?" he asked.

"Yes, but if we come back here at 2 o'clock our time we'll be okay as we haven't seen the girls in a few hours, so they won't see us or our other selves and notice the difference," I said. "So, we'll go home and get some lunch, then when we come back we can spend the rest of the day with them and try to enjoy what time we have left here."

"Okay, then," he said. "Let's go."

We quickly got changed, locked up the den, and made our way to the magic door. Then, being careful not to be spotted by Sean or David as we knew they were out looking for us, we crept through the grass to the other side.

"Coast's clear," I said. "Let's go home and get some lunch."

As we walked down through the village we noticed a car outside Paul's house - but more noticeable was that his door was a different colour from what I remembered.

"That's strange, Thomas!" I said.

I didn't need to tell him what I was talking about; he'd already seen it for himself. He nodded.

Worried, we went to call on him.

The door opened and, to our surprise, a strange lady stood there.

"Hello, boys, what can I do for you?"

Confused, we asked if Paul could come out to play.

"Paul?" she said. "I don't know any Paul!"

I looked at Thomas, stepped back, and looked at the house. "We are at the right door, aren't we?" I asked.

"Yes," he said slowly.

"Are you both okay?" the lady asked. "You look a little lost!"

"Our friend Paul lives here!" Thomas blurted out.

"I'm sorry, boys," she said. "You must have the wrong house. I've lived here for over 30 years and there's never been a Paul here! Sorry I can't help you more, goodbye." And with that she closed the door.

We both walked down the path, confused and unsure of what had just happened. We stood at the gate, uncertain what to do. Just then we saw my aunt Emma on her way to my grandma and grandad's.

"Hello, boys," she said. "You look confused. Anything wrong?"

"Yes, we're looking for Paul," I said. "That lady says he doesn't live there."

"Paul?" Auntie Emma asked, puzzled. "I've never heard you mention a friend called Paul before."

"Never mind," I said, grabbing Thomas by the arm and dragging him back towards the quarry.

"What's going on?" he asked.

"I must have changed something dramatic in the past when I got caught talking to Elsa," I said, as we ran. "Her mum was furious!"

"I remember Elsa telling us earlier this week that her mum would send her to a boarding school if she ever got caught talking to boys," Thomas said anxiously.

"She must've been telling the truth!" I cried. "She must've been sent home and we've completely altered the entire future and erased Paul from existence!"

"What are we going to do?" he asked, aghast.

"We need to get back to Elsa's village as quickly as possible and stop my other self from going up to her house," I panted. "It's the only way to stop the events that erase Paul's entire life out of existence. But we need to hurry, we only have a few hours!"

Without getting changed or checking that the coast was clear, we went through the magic door. Since we needed to be sure that we didn't bump into the girls as we needed to do this without them knowing, we didn't go anywhere near the den.

Even though we were tired and hungry, we ran as fast as we could towards Elsa's village. There wasn't a minute to spare. Hiding in the play area, we got our breath back from the exhausting run.

"How are we going to do this, then?" Thomas asked.

"You need to go down near Elsa's house, but stay out of sight, and when you see the other me walking towards the house you'll have to go and stop me," I told him. "You'll need to explain what's going on and I'll have to stay here. It's broad daylight. Nobody can see both of us on the same road at the same time."

It was going to be tricky, but it needed to be done and it needed to be done now, as we'd never get another chance to save Paul. We couldn't leave things as they were.

As I was fretting about whether or not it would work, Thomas said, "Duck! Look over there! I can see you walking into the village!"

I peered through the leaves. It was incredibly weird, seeing myself walking down the road.

"Stay there!" Thomas said, as he ran over to my other self.

"George!" I heard him shout.

I hunkered down in the bushes, trying to stay out of sight as I watched them talking to each other.

"What you are doing here, Thomas?" my other self asked, surprised. "I thought you were going straight to the den to meet the girls."

Thomas grabbed my arm and pulled me aside. "What's wrong?" the other me asked. "Why are you looking so worried?"

"Just come with me!" he said, pulling me around the back of the houses and out of sight of the road.

I couldn't hear them talking anymore, but I was beginning to remember the conversation, even though I knew I hadn't been there. It was peculiar. It made me feel a little ill.

I remembered Thomas telling me about Paul and what we had to do. I remembered being confused, but agreeing to hide outside the village so Elsa didn't see me. I remembered Thomas saying that we had to go back and see if it had worked.

"It has to work!" I said to myself. "It just has to!"

I felt a strange tugging sensation and then I was crouching in the bushes outside of town and not in the play area. Confused, I fell backwards until I was sitting down.

"What?" I whispered, astonished.

I heard sudden footsteps on the road. Suddenly, Thomas appeared.

I shouted to him. "Over here!"

"Why are you hiding here?" he asked, as soon as he was under cover. "You're supposed to be avoiding your other self!"

"I think I am my other self," I said, feeling dazed.

I told him what had happened, and about the feeling of being in two places at once.

"And then I was here."

Thomas put his head in his hands. "None of this makes sense," he groaned. "Time travel hurts my head."

"We'd better get back to the den before Elsa sees us," I said sadly.

Our hiding place was on the far side of the church, so we had to cross on the other side of the street to Elsa's house. As we were leaving, I looked back and saw her at the door, watching us walk away. She looked hurt and confused. It broke my heart seeing the look on her face.

"Don't even think about it!" Thomas warned me. He saw my eyes well up and grabbed my arm, making sure I stayed on track.

As soon as we got back to our village we headed to the quarry and then straight to the magic door to see if our plan had worked.

"Coast clear!" I said. "Let's go straight to Paul's house to see if we've fixed it!"

We ran the whole way, and when we arrived we noticed his door was back to the same dark grey it had always been and there was no car outside. Feeling some relief, we stood at his gate, wondering how we could confirm that Paul was okay before he came home from holiday.

Auntie Emma walked past on the way back from her errands. "Are you okay, boys?" she asked.

"Yes," I said. "We're just looking to see if Paul's in."

I held my breath in case she said she didn't know who he was, but she just frowned at us.

"Isn't he still on holiday?"

Thomas and I both let out a sigh of relief. My legs felt a little weak and I almost fell to the ground, I was that exhausted from excitement, emotion, and fear. I managed to stay upright, however.

"Oh, yes," I managed to say. "You're right, Auntie Emma. I just forgot."

"You'd forget your head if it wasn't screwed on!" she said fondly. She walked away, laughing.

"We did it!" I said, leaning against the wall. "Mission accomplished!"

"What now?" Thomas asked, looking similarly worn out.

"Well, I don't think we can risk going down to the den," I said. I rubbed my hand over my face. "Everything seems to be falling apart. The old lady in the tent was right. We're in danger and we need to stop doing what we're doing."

I sighed. "We need to go back tomorrow to save my dad's life and then that's it!" I said. "You can say goodbye to Iris and once I've completed that mission I'll come and get you and we'll leave the magic door behind forever."

Thomas nodded. "You won't get any arguments from me. I'll miss Iris very much, but we can't risk changing the future like that again."

We spent the rest of the day playing on the rope swing, trying not to think about how close we'd come to losing our best friend forever. We went over the plan time and time again to make sure we'd thought of everything.

We couldn't afford to be reckless. I had to save my dad's life, or me, Sean, and David would cease to exist.

Chapter Twenty-Three

The Truth

After breakfast I met Thomas outside at 8:30.

"You ready?" I asked.

"Yes," he replied with a sigh. "Ready as I'll ever be."

For the last time, we made our way down towards the magic door. By the time we got there our nerves were shot to bits.

"We need to go through and then go straight to the den," I said, "so we can say goodbye."

We crawled through, but on the far side, Thomas said, "I was almost certain I heard Sean shouting David's name just then."

"Don't worry about it!" I said. "After today we won't be coming back down here again, so there'll be nothing for them to find out!"

We went over to the den to wait for the girls, but when we got there, they were already there.

Iris and Aly popped their heads out from around the door and Aly said, "Nice of you both to turn up! Better late than never. You were supposed to meet us here last night."

"Sorry!" Thomas apologised. "Something came up - an emergency. We had to go home."

"Well, you're here now," she said, as Iris took his arm. "So, what shall we do?"

"I can only stay for one hour," I said. "I have to go and meet my friend John. I promised him we'd hang out together today."

Just then Thomas said, "You can both come with me and play around the quarry if you like?"

"Alright," said Iris. "I'd like that."

We spent a bittersweet hour playing in the den and working in the allotment until it was time to go, and far too soon, the hour was up.

"I need to go now," I said, trying not to cry. I was very sad knowing that this was the last time I'd see the girls at the age they were. I threw my arms around both Iris and Aly and give them a big hug and a kiss on the cheek.

"What's up with you?" Aly asked, baffled and concerned. "You'd think you were going away forever, the way you're going on!"

I could tell from her expression that deep down she knew something was wrong; she just couldn't put her finger on what it was.

"Nothing's up," I said, quickly turning away before I started crying as I walked out of the den for the very last time.

Thomas followed me out, looking similarly upset. "All set?" he asked.

"Yes! All set. I'll see you when we get home tonight." I shook his hand and then pulled him in for a hug, worried that I might not see him again either.

"Don't panic," he told me. "Just remember the plan and stay calm when you fall in the water - you'll be fine."

I made my way down towards the quarry to travel back to 1986 where I intended to grab the raft and travel back to 1966 to help save Dad's life.

Knowing that Thomas had heard Sean shouting earlier, I crawled along on my belly to the other side of the door, but luckily my brothers were nowhere to be seen.

I crept around the quarry to where we'd hidden the raft. From there I could hear them playing down by the rope swing. I knew I had to be extra careful and quick, so they wouldn't catch me.

I quickly uncovered the raft and climbed aboard, then I started making my way towards the middle of the water to door number 2. I took a quick look around before passing through. Just as I passed through the door I heard Sean shout my name, but I couldn't see him. It was too late; I'd passed through onto the other side.

I knew that what I had to do was far more important than him seeing me disappear right now. I'd just have to worry about that later.

I paddled the raft ashore, leaving it on the side of the bank before going over to the quarry wall to sit and wait for John.

I didn't have to wait for long; soon I saw him walking over with the rope under his arm.

"Morning George!" he said. "Have you been here long?"

"No!" I said. "Just got here myself, and I've not seen any police kicking about, so we should be okay."

I was surprised at how steady my voice was considering the dread I felt.

"Come on, then!" he said. "Let's get this done."

I climbed down, tying one end of the rope to an old piece of metal bar that was poking out of the crumbling wall, while Dad tied off the other end, making the rope tight against the wall.

"Right," he said, "are you ready to do this? We'll be the first people to shimmy across the water from one side to the other!"

I bit my lip and looked over to the other side of quarry to see if I could see Thomas, Iris, or Aly, but I couldn't see them - not yet.

"Hold on!" I said, trying to stall him until they got there.

"What?" he asked.

"We need to make a plan for who's doing what," I said uncertainly.

To my relief, at that moment I saw Thomas appear on the far side of the quarry with Iris and Aly.

"Make a plan?" John laughed. "We're only walking along a rope. It's not rocket science!"

With Thomas and the girls in place, I knew it was time. My hands were shaking. My legs felt like jelly. I turned and looked at Thomas and the girls, giving them a wave. They waved back. I knew it was time. There was no going back, now.

I was steeling myself, but before I could even think about what was about to happen, I heard John yelp and give a shout. My head whipped around. My dad had lost his grip on the rope and was just about clinging on.

With my heart in my mouth, I reached down and stretched my arm out as far as I could. He also stretched his up to me as far he could reach, and we managed to grab each other by the hand.

"Hold on!" I said. "I'll try to pull you up."

I pulled as hard as I could and he started to climb back up the wall.

I thought, *This is it! I've got him!*

After a moment he managed to get his feet onto a protruding ledge on the quarry wall.

John shouted "I'm okay!" and immediately I lost my footing, slipped, fell, and banged my head really hard against the wall surface.

Stunned, and with my head swimming, I fell head first into the water.

The blow to my head had been far harder than I was expecting, and I thought I was going to pass out; I could see stars. The water was freezing cold. It closed around my chest like a fist, making me seize up.

I curled up into a ball, making sure I held my breath. I knew I had to compose myself John see me sink out of sight before I tried to swim to safety. From beneath the surface I could hear him shouting my name.

"George!" he yelled frantically, over and over again.

The shouts became quieter and quieter as I sank deeper and the water grew colder and darker.

This wasn't the plan. My thoughts felt sluggish and dark. I could barely move. The reality was that I was actually drowning. I started to panic, thinking it was all over. I had saved my dad's life, but in return I was dying.

It had all gone horribly wrong, I thought, as I felt myself drifting off, sinking deeper and deeper under the surface.

Just when I thought there was no hope I felt someone grab my arm and pull me up. I found myself sitting in a puddle only a few of feet deep. There were two girls helping me to my feet. They supported me and helped me walk up to the ridge above an old, dried up quarry.

One asked, "What are you doing, lying down in a two-foot puddle of water? Trying to kill yourself?"

"No, I just fell in!" I said. "I hit my head, but… I'm confused, where's all the water from the quarry?"

"Maybe that bang on your head has made you forget how you got there?" the other girl suggested, giving me an odd look.

"Maybe." I raised my hand to my aching head and it came back covered in blood. I felt dizzy and disoriented. "Who are you?"

"I'm Abby and this is my younger sister, Holly," said the first girl. "We're from the village."

"What about you? What's your name?" Holly asked.

"George," I said, confused. "What happened to the water?" I asked again.

"It was drained years ago, after a young boy drowned here back in 1986," Abby explained.

"1986?" I asked. "Don't you mean 1966? The boy called George?"

"No," she said. "That was my grandad's friend. No, the boy who died in 1986 was called Thomas, our dad's best friend."

My mouth fell open in complete shock. I was in the future! And Thomas -

Oh, no!

He must have jumped into the water to save me.

"What's wrong?" Holly asked, worried. "Are you okay? You look like you've just seen a ghost."

"I need to go!" I shouted. "I need to go home, I need to find out what happened to Thomas! this can't be happening!"

In a panic, I ran as fast as I could back towards the magic door. I ran through the puddle the girls pulled me from, I fell as I reached the puddle. From behind me I heard them shout, "No!"

Then I was in the water again, sinking deeper and deeper. I tried to swim, but I couldn't. I struggled, but it was no use. Everything went dark and I must have passed out for a second. Just then I felt myself being shaken and heard my name being shouted. It was Sean.

"George!" he shouted. "George, are you okay?"

I opened my eyes. Everything was blurry. I felt sick.

"I must have fallen over and banged my head," I murmured.

"Where is Thomas?" he asked, panic in his voice. "Where is he?"

"I don't know," I said, suddenly remembering what the girls from the future said.

"We saw you and him both in the water," he said.

"No!" I shouted. "No!" I struggled to my feet, my clothes soaking wet. I was still bleeding from the cut on my head. "He can't have fallen in!"

I heard shouting, and David ran up, leading our parents - and Thomas's. He must have run off to find them while Sean tried to pull me out.

"Thomas is in the water!" Sean yelled. "I can't see him!"

Thomas's mum screamed.

I clutched my head. This could not be happening.

Everyone was screaming and shouting for Thomas. I felt I could barely stand. Sean stayed beside me, one hand on my shoulder.

They circled the quarry, searching along the bank, but Thomas was nowhere to be found.

I could hear Thomas's mum screaming and crying. "Thomas! He's gone! He's drowned! My beautiful little boy," she wept as she fell to her knees.

I felt numb all over. I couldn't believe what was happening. Thomas was dead. I was never going to see him again.

"George!" she shouted, pain and fury etched onto her face. "We told you not to play down here! Thomas has drowned and it's all your fault!"

I could not believe what I was hearing, but she was right. It *was* all my fault.

I put my head in my hands, collapsed to the ground, and started to cry. I couldn't believe he'd drowned. It felt like I'd killed my best friend in the whole world.

I heard Dad say, "Take George home."

Sean and David helped me to my feet and started walking me home. I looked over my shoulder at the search party, still looking frantically for my friend, and stumbled.

"We'll take you to Grandad and Grandma's house," David said kindly. "Then we'll come back down and help find your friend."

"Thank you," I replied through my tears.

When we got to Grandma and Grandad's, Grandad was standing at the door waiting for me.

"Are you okay, George?" he asked.

"No! My friend, my best friend Thomas, he's fallen in the water and drowned and it's all my fault," I sobbed.

"Come in and sit down with me and your grandma," he said, leading me inside. "Let her look at that bump on your head."

He wrapped a large towel around me to keep me warm.

"I'm not bothered about the bump on my head," I said. "I just want to find my friend. I need to go back and help them find him. You don't understand!"

"No! You need to stay here and get cleaned up," he said firmly. "So, go and sit in the living room and Grandma will get you some dry clothes and make you some food."

Grandma cleaned the cut on my head, then kissed me and went into the kitchen. Grandad came back in with some jam and toast before sitting down on the chair opposite me.

"Do you want to talk, George?" Grandad asked.

"I don't know, I guess so."

He moved over to me on the settee, looked at me, and said, "Did you ever wonder why I was always there to help you out, like when I gave you the watch?" he asked. "Or why I made the wooden box and kept all that money for you? Or why I love Patch so much?"

"No," I said, sniffling, "what's this got to do with anything? Thomas drowned! I don't understand."

Grandad smiled sadly and took my hand. "Let me tell you a little story about when I was your age and I used to play out with my best friends."

I thought he was doing this to take my mind off what had just happened to Thomas. I didn't really want to listen to the story - I was too sad - but it was my grandad, so I sat there and listened, not really paying attention.

"Some of the best days of my life were when I was a little boy about your age," he told me. "I was always playing with my best friends on the rope swing and down at the quarry. We would play for hours and hours, throwing stones into the water at plastic bottles." He smiled. "We used to play down the quarry even though our dads wouldn't allow us. We thought we were clever and we came up with a cunning plan to make the rope swing. One day we even nearly burned down the woods, trying to make a map."

I frowned. That was familiar.

Grandad put his hand on my shoulder and passed me the photo from the opening day of the Co-Op.

"This is me," he said, pointing himself out. "And this was my best friend in the whole world."

He was pointing at Thomas and me. I was confused. Maybe the bang on my head had been worse than I thought. I stared at him. Grandad pulled something out of his pocket: it was the watch he'd given me a few weeks before. The same watch I gave Thomas to look after, only now it looked old and scruffy.

I took one look at it and went ice-cold. I looked up at my grandad's face, shocked.

"Remember? We had the best time in the world when you found that magic door!" he said, a smile on his face.

For the first time in my life I saw Thomas in his face, as clear as day.

"Thomas?" I whispered to my grandad. "Is that really you?"

My heart was pumping at over 100 miles per hour.

Grandad smiled. "Yes George, it's me, Thomas."

My head still spinning, I threw my arms around his neck.

"But how?" I asked. I had so many questions. "What happened? How are you here? I thought your name was Den?"

"That's what your grandma nicknamed me, because she found me living in the den. We agreed never to tell you my real name, because we couldn't risk you working out that I was your grandad, so we kept it from you that my name was really Thomas."

"Grandma knows?"

"Everything," he said. "I had to tell her. She was so upset the day see you drown."

"But… how?" I asked. "What happened back then?"

He sat back in his chair. "Fifty years ago, when we went back in time to say goodbye to the girls and you went off to save your dad, we went to the quarry. We saw you across the water.

"I saw him slip. In horror, I watched you fall in and I kept hoping you'd pop back up, but you never did. I panicked and jumped in myself, swimming over to where you went under. I could see John, but I couldn't pass through to help you. I thought you'd drowned.

"On the bank, Iris and Aly saw John jump in the water looking for you, but shortly after, the hazy doors disappeared too, and the girls thought you'd both drowned."

He rubbed a hand over his face.

"So, that's where the story of two boys drowning in 1936 came from John and me?" I asked.

"Yes," he said. "While I was swimming in there, looking for you, Sean and David must have been able to see through the magic doors. They saw you go under. I couldn't get back, so I slipped out of sight, back into 1936. They must have thought I'd gone under the water as well and drowned.

"Your dad thought you'd drowned, too. I'll never forget the day he came running home to us, distraught. But the fact of the matter is that no one has ever died in the quarry!"

"What happened to you after I went?" I said.

"It was the hardest time of my life," he told me. "I didn't know if you'd drowned or not, but you never came back for me. I ended up living in the den, with the money we had there. I would go down to the magic door every day hoping and wishing that you'd come back for me. Eventually, I thought you must have died or someone had stopped you, because I couldn't imagine you just leaving me there.

"Iris came to see me every day," he went on. "She knew I was hungry and would bring rations of food: bread, potatoes, and carrots, while we waited for our vegetables to grow. She noticed that I'd become more and more untidy and scruffy and finally she asked why I wasn't going home so I had to tell her the truth. I thought she'd think I was mad, but she didn't."

He grinned. "She looked at me as if she had always known and just took care of me. She was my world."

She walked in then. "Hello, old friend," she said with a smile, pulling me into a hug.

I sat between them on the sofa.

"As the years passed and we grew older, your grandma and I truly fell in love," he said. "It was almost like destiny wanted us to be together. She was the most amazing person in the world to me. As soon as we were old enough, we got married and had a little boy we named John. We both knew that when he was 10 years old he would meet his son - you!"

"And then your mum and dad grew up and had you," Grandma explained.

"The day John brought you around our house after playing down the quarry I couldn't believe my eyes," Grandad said. "I had to leave the room. It was the first time I had seen you since the day I see you go under the water, I ran off to my bedroom and cried like a little boy. You were my best friend, but I couldn't tell you. It was the first time I'd seen you in 20 years."

They both put an arm around my shoulders.

"Your grandma came upstairs," he continued. "She was the only one who knew why I was crying and who you were. It took me nearly ten minutes to compose myself and come down, I wanted to tell you everything, but obviously I couldn't."

"We knew, as soon as John came home the day he thought he saw you drown, that it was truly you. For us, the pain of knowing what was going to happen to you was unbearable. We still had no way of knowing if you'd drowned. Not until recently." "Recently?" I asked but didn't follow up.

"Wait a minute!" I shouted as I stood up. "I've got it! Why don't I just go back now and get you, and bring you back home? You know now I didn't drown."

"No!" they both shouted at once. Iris added, "You can't and must not ever try!"

"When I told you that I thought you were either dead or that someone must have stopped you from coming back for me," said Grandad, "well… that was me, right now. You see, if you go back and change things now, you, Sean, David, John - none of you will ever be born.

I looked at my grandad and realised he was right. My 10-year-old friend Thomas was really gone forever, but he was also standing in front of me as an old man. I put my head in my hands and cried. I was sad, relieved, confused, and missing my friend, all at once.

"I'm going to have to pretend to my mum, my dad, and everyone else that you died," I said. "Even mum and dad."

Apart from Paul I could never tell anyone the secret; I would have to live the rest of my life with everyone thinking that my best friend Thomas had died and that it was my fault.

"The main thing is that you're here and alright," he said. "Safe and sound at home. And it was my choice to join you in the past, so it isn't all your fault. I will tell people that I heard Thomas ask you to play at the quarry." He nodded his head. "It's going to be hard watching my parents grieve, but I'll make sure they're alright." His face brightened up. "There's so much I want to tell you - things I couldn't tell you before today."

"Did you ever find out who the strange man was who saved my life and signed for the allotment?" I asked, my mind still muddled.

"In time," he said. "In time!" He changed the subject. "How long were you in the water after we saw you fall in?"

"Well," I said, "after you saw me fall in, I was pulled out of a two-foot-deep puddle of water."

I told him that the water in the quarry would be drained next year to prevent anyone else from drowning after today, and I also told him about the girls I met.

He sat up, excited.

"Another magic door!" Grandma Iris gasped. "That makes sense."

"What does?" I asked.

"Oh, nothing," he replied. "Nothing to worry about."

I had the strangest feeling that he wasn't telling me everything, but after the day I'd had I could hardly bring myself to care. All that mattered was that we were both alright after a sort. I sat there wondering would there be more adventuring for me?.

"Is this it, then?" I asked, a little disappointed. "Is our time travelling really over?"

My grandad and best friend smiled. "Only time will tell, my friend! Only time will tell!" …

The Origins of the Story

George is, in fact, me: Gavin Hodgson. Thomas and Paul are the characters of my friends back then, and they still are my friends today - over 35 years later. Iris, Alice, and Em were actually my Grandma and great aunties and Grandad was called Thomas all of which I wanted to immortalise in this book.

When I was younger - long before they died - they used to tell me stories of the things they used to get up to, things that weren't too dissimilar to what I was getting up to at the time. So, all I did was join our two worlds together by using the magic door and adding in some extra twists and turns. All the adventures the characters get up to in the book, across all generations - including my dad's during his childhood - were close to the truth.

The quarry in the book was actually locally named 'the drift'. The oak tree in the woods that swung over the stream was actually real, and it adjoined the drift. We used to sneak 'down town' (which was really 'up town' from where we lived), and we also used to have an allotment complete with old shed where we would hide out when it rained. The yellow wellies in the greenhouse were part of my attire for a short time when playing down the drift. And the school at the bottom of the village was used as the coal board offices before it was knocked down in the early 80's

All of the generations grew up in the same village, and as the playgrounds were still the same, writing the story came easy to me. It was also a great way to recall the memories of my late great grandparents and aunties.

Coming Up...

George's Generations: Once Upon A Timeline

What happened to Granddad in 1936? Who was the strange man who kept helping the boys out? And what happened when George met Paul's grandma after Thomas was seen to be drowned?

Continue the story of George's antics as he and his dad play around the quarry, discover the unknown dangers they're forced to dice with, and learn how the adventure can never end as George, Thomas, and Paul battle to keep the existence of their whole family safe for generations to come, as the story continues...

GEORGE'S GENERATIONS: THROUGH THE MAGIC DOORS

George's Generations is the first book written by author Gavin Hodgson, the successful inventor of the Saturn Eazyfile, as seen on TV.

You can find out more information about George's Generations, its future sequels, and the author at www.gavinhodgson.co.uk

30740886R00201

Printed in Great
Britain
by Amazon